**ENVIRONMENTAL REMEDIATION TECHNOLOGIES, REGULATIONS AND SAFETY**



# THE NATIONAL ENVIRONMENTAL POLICY ACT

## BACKGROUND, COSTS AND BENEFITS OF NEPA ANALYSES

# ENVIRONMENTAL REMEDIATION TECHNOLOGIES, REGULATIONS AND SAFETY

Additional books in this series can be found on Nova's website under the Series tab.

Additional e-books in this series can be found on Nova's website under the e-book tab.

ENVIRONMENTAL REMEDIATION TECHNOLOGIES, REGULATIONS AND SAFETY

# THE NATIONAL ENVIRONMENTAL POLICY ACT

## BACKGROUND, COSTS AND BENEFITS OF NEPA ANALYSES

SABRINA REYNOLDS
EDITOR

*New York*

For permission to use material from this book please contact us:
Telephone 631-231-7269; Fax 631-231-8175
Web Site: http://www.novapublishers.com



**Library of Congress Cataloging-in-Publication Data**

ISBN: 978-1-63321-464-4

*Published by Nova Science Publishers, Inc. † New York*

# CONTENTS

# PREFACE

The goals of the National Environmental Policy Act are to declare a national environmental policy, provide federal agencies with action-forcing provisions intended to ensure that the goals of the policy are implemented, establish the Council on Environmental Quality (CEQ) to provide advice to the President on environmental matters and to monitor the state of the environment, and require the President to submit to Congress an annual report on the state of the environment. This book describes information on the number and type of NEPA analyses; costs and benefits of completing those analyses; and frequency and outcomes of related litigation.

Chapter 1 – Beginning in the late 1950s and through the 1960s, Congress reacted to increasing public concern about the impact that human activity could have on the environment. A key legislative option to address this concern was the declaration of a national environmental policy. Advocates of this approach argued that without a specific policy, federal agencies were neither able nor inclined to consider the environmental impacts of their actions in fulfilling the agency's mission. The statute that ultimately addressed this issue was the National Environmental Policy Act of 1969 (NEPA, 42 U.S.C. §§ 4321-4347).

Signed into law by President Nixon on January 1, 1970, NEPA was the first of several major environmental laws passed in the 1970s. It declared a national policy to protect the environment and created a Council on Environmental Quality (CEQ) in the Executive Office of the President. To implement the national policy, NEPA required that a detailed statement of environmental impacts be prepared for all major federal actions significantly affecting the environment. The "detailed statement" would ultimately be referred to as an environmental impact statement (EIS).

With an initial absence of regulations specifying implementation procedures and no agency authorized to enforce the law, federal agencies reacted in different ways to NEPA's requirements. Some had difficulty complying with the law's EIS requirements. As a result, litigation that served to interpret NEPA's requirements and enforce agency compliance began almost immediately. In addition to questions of procedure (e.g., how, when, or why an EIS must be prepared), another question was how the environmental policy goals of the act should be implemented or enforced. The courts ultimately decided that NEPA is a procedural statute with twin aims requiring agencies to (1) consider the environmental impacts of their proposed actions and (2) inform the public that they (the agencies) considered environmental concerns in their decision-making process. In that capacity, NEPA has become a primary mechanism for public participation in the federal decision-making process.

As it has been implemented, most agencies use NEPA as an "umbrella" statute. As such, NEPA forms a framework to coordinate or demonstrate compliance with any study, review, or consultation required by other environmental laws. The use of NEPA in this capacity can lead to confusion. The need to comply with another environmental law, such as the Clean Water Act, may be identified within the framework of the NEPA process, but NEPA itself is not the source of the obligation. Theoretically, if the requirement to comply with NEPA were removed, compliance with each applicable law would still be required.

Chapter 2 – NEPA requires all federal agencies to evaluate the potential environmental effects of proposed projects—such as roads or bridges—on the human environment. Agencies prepare an EIS when a project will have a potentially significant impact on the environment. They may prepare an EA to determine whether a project will have a significant potential impact. If a project fits within a category of activities determined to have no significant impact—a CE— then an EA or an EIS is generally not necessary. The adequacy of these analyses has been a focus of litigation.

GAO was asked to review various issues associated with completing NEPA analyses. This report describes information on the (1) number and type of NEPA analyses, (2) costs and benefits of completing those analyses, and (3) frequency and outcomes of related litigation. GAO included available information on both costs and benefits to be consistent with standard economic principles for evaluating federal programs, and selected the Departments of Defense, Energy, the Interior, and Transportation, and the USDA Forest Service for analysis because they generally complete the most NEPA analyses.

GAO reviewed documents and interviewed individuals from federal agencies, academia, and professional groups with expertise in NEPA analyses and litigation. GAO's findings are not generalizeable to agencies other than those selected.

This report has no recommendations. GAO provided a draft to CEQ and agency officials for review and comment, and they generally agreed with GAO's findings.

In: The National Environmental Policy Act ISBN: 978-1-63321-464-4
Editor: Sabrina Reynolds 

*Chapter 1*

# THE NATIONAL ENVIRONMENTAL POLICY ACT (NEPA): BACKGROUND AND IMPLEMENTATION*

*Linda Luther*

## SUMMARY

Beginning in the late 1950s and through the 1960s, Congress reacted to increasing public concern about the impact that human activity could have on the environment. A key legislative option to address this concern was the declaration of a national environmental policy. Advocates of this approach argued that without a specific policy, federal agencies were neither able nor inclined to consider the environmental impacts of their actions in fulfilling the agency's mission. The statute that ultimately addressed this issue was the National Environmental Policy Act of 1969 (NEPA, 42 U.S.C. §§ 4321-4347).

Signed into law by President Nixon on January 1, 1970, NEPA was the first of several major environmental laws passed in the 1970s. It declared a national policy to protect the environment and created a Council on Environmental Quality (CEQ) in the Executive Office of the President. To implement the national policy, NEPA required that a detailed statement of environmental impacts be prepared for all major federal actions significantly affecting the environment. The "detailed

---

* This is an edited, reformatted and augmented version of Congressional Research Service Report RL33152, dated January 10, 2011.

statement" would ultimately be referred to as an environmental impact statement (EIS).

With an initial absence of regulations specifying implementation procedures and no agency authorized to enforce the law, federal agencies reacted in different ways to NEPA's requirements. Some had difficulty complying with the law's EIS requirements. As a result, litigation that served to interpret NEPA's requirements and enforce agency compliance began almost immediately. In addition to questions of procedure (e.g., how, when, or why an EIS must be prepared), another question was how the environmental policy goals of the act should be implemented or enforced. The courts ultimately decided that NEPA is a procedural statute with twin aims requiring agencies to (1) consider the environmental impacts of their proposed actions and (2) inform the public that they (the agencies) considered environmental concerns in their decision-making process. In that capacity, NEPA has become a primary mechanism for public participation in the federal decision-making process.

As it has been implemented, most agencies use NEPA as an "umbrella" statute. As such, NEPA forms a framework to coordinate or demonstrate compliance with any study, review, or consultation required by other environmental laws. The use of NEPA in this capacity can lead to confusion. The need to comply with another environmental law, such as the Clean Water Act, may be identified within the framework of the NEPA process, but NEPA itself is not the source of the obligation. Theoretically, if the requirement to comply with NEPA were removed, compliance with each applicable law would still be required.

## INTRODUCTION

Prior to the 1960s, little formal consideration was given to the potential impact of human activity on the environment. Beginning in the late 1950s and into the 1960s, the public became increasingly aware of and concerned about those impacts. During that time, Members of Congress debated the need for a national policy on the environment and for an Executive-level council or committee that could provide advice to the President on environmental policy issues. The statute that ultimately addressed these needs was the National Environmental Policy Act of 1969 (NEPA, 42 U.S.C. §§ 4321-4347).

Signed into law by President Nixon on January 1, 1970, NEPA was the first of several major environmental laws passed in the 1970s. It declared a national policy to protect the environment. To implement its policy, NEPA requires federal agencies to provide a detailed statement of environmental impacts, subsequently referred to as an environmental impact statement (EIS), for every recommendation or report on proposals for legislation and other major federal action *significantly* affecting the quality of the human environment.

The act also created the Council on Environmental Quality (CEQ) in the Executive Office of the President. Among other duties, CEQ provides oversight of NEPA's implementation. In 1978, CEQ was authorized by executive order to issue regulations applicable to all federal agencies regarding the preparation of EISs. However, CEQ was not authorized to enforce those regulations.

As it was subsequently interpreted, NEPA is a procedural statute with two primary aims. First, it obligates federal agencies to consider every significant aspect of the environmental impact of an action *before* proceeding with it. Second, it ensures that the agency responsible for the action will inform the public what the action is and that it has considered environmental concerns in its decision-making process. In this capacity, NEPA has become one of the primary mechanisms through which the public is able to participate in the federal decision-making process.

As a procedural statute, NEPA does not require agencies to elevate environmental concerns above others. Instead, NEPA requires only that the agency assess the environmental consequences of an action and its alternatives before proceeding. If the adverse environmental effects of the proposed action are adequately identified and evaluated, the agency is not constrained by NEPA from deciding that other benefits outweigh the environmental costs and moving forward with the action.

Most agencies use NEPA as an umbrella statute—that is, a framework to coordinate or demonstrate compliance with any studies, reviews, or consultations required by any other environmental laws. The use of NEPA in this capacity can lead to confusion. The need to comply with another environmental law, such as the Clean Water Act or Endangered Species Act, may be identified within the framework of the NEPA process, but NEPA itself is not the source of the obligation. Theoretically, if the requirement to comply with NEPA were removed, compliance with each applicable law would still be required.

Unlike other environment-related statutes, no individual agency has enforcement authority with regard to NEPA's environmental review requirements.[1] This absence of enforcement authority is sometimes cited as the reason that litigation has been chosen as an avenue by individuals and groups that disagree with how an agency meets NEPA's mandate or EIS requirements for a given project. (For example, a group may charge that an EIS is inadequate or that the environmental impacts of an action will in fact be significant when an agency claims they are not). Critics of NEPA charge that those who disapprove of a federal project will use NEPA as the basis for litigation to delay or halt that project. Others argue that litigation only results when agencies do not comply with NEPA's procedural requirements.

Environmental groups often refer to NEPA as the "Magna Carta" of environmental law. They view it as an essential tool to help agencies plan and manage federal actions in a responsible way by requiring policymakers and project sponsors to consider the environmental implications of their actions before decisions are made. Environmental groups also view the NEPA process as an important mechanism in providing the public with an opportunity to be involved in agency planning efforts. Critics charge that the law creates a complicated array of regulations and logistical delays that stall agency action.

This report provides information about NEPA's background and legislative history, provisions of the law, the role of the courts and CEQ in its implementation, how agencies implement NEPA's requirements, how the public is involved in the NEPA process, the means by which NEPA is used as an umbrella statute to coordinate or demonstrate compliance with other environmental requirements, and claims by some stakeholders that NEPA causes delays in some federal actions.

## NEPA and Its History

In the 1950s and 1960s, Congress began to react to increasing public concern about the environment. In the congressional debates that ensued, a key legislative option considered was the declaration of a national environmental policy. Such a policy would require all federal agencies, whose actions were often seen as significant sources of pollution, to adhere to certain environmental values and goals. Advocates of a national policy argued that without a specific environmental policy, federal agencies were neither able nor inclined to consider the environmental impacts of their actions in fulfilling the agency's mission. Debate also existed regarding the creation of an Executive-level board or council that would gather information regarding the state of the environment and provide environmental policy advice to the President.

## Background and Legislative History

For at least 10 years before NEPA was enacted, Congress debated issues that the act would ultimately address. The act was modeled on the Resources and Conservation Act of 1959, introduced by Senator James E. Murray in the 86th Congress. That bill would have established an environmental advisory counsel in the office of the President, declared a national environmental policy, and required the preparation of an annual environmental report.[2]

In the years following the introduction of Senator Murray's bill, similar bills were introduced and hearings were held to discuss the state of the environment and Congress's potential responses to perceived problems. In 1968, a joint House-Senate colloquium was convened by the chairmen of the Senate Committee on Interior and Insular Affairs (Senator Henry Jackson) and the House Committee on Science and Astronautics (Representative George Miller) to discuss the need for and potential means of implementing a national environmental policy. In the colloquium, some Members of Congress expressed a continuing concern over federal agency actions affecting the environment. Governor Laurence Rockefeller, a participant in the colloquium, stated before the joint committee:

> [W]e do not have a clearly stated national attitude toward the environment. In the areas of civil rights, education, full employment, and a number of others, the Congress of the United States has set forth a clearly understood national policy. This lack of overall national policy has been reflected in recent action of the courts in reversing decisions of administrative agencies on the grounds that they did not give sufficient consideration to environmental factors. Clearly, these agencies need better guidelines.[3]

Many of the concepts and ideas drawn from this colloquium would ultimately form the basis for the bills that would become NEPA. For example, in discussing new approaches to government, Senator Jackson argued that new approaches to environmental management were required, and he urged the colloquium to provide thoughts on possible "action-forcing" processes that could be put into operation.[4] The discussion of action-forcing processes to implement a national policy provided the seeds of the idea that would eventually become the requirement to prepare an environmental impact statement.

The bills that would become NEPA were introduced in the Senate and House in 1969 by Senator Jackson and Representative John Dingell.[5] In introducing the Senate bill, Senator Jackson stated that its purpose was to "lay the framework for a continuing program of research and study which will insure that present and future generations of Americans will be able to live in and enjoy an environment free of hazards to mental and physical well-being."[6] To accomplish this end, the Senate bill authorized federal agencies to conduct investigations and gather data on environmental issues. The bill also established a Council on Environmental Quality to analyze and study the information gathered and to advise and assist the President in the formulation of national policies.

The Senate Committee on Interior and Insular Affairs held a hearing on the proposed bills[7] in April 1969. During the hearing, the concept of creating some action-forcing mechanism, as a means of implementing a national environmental policy, was again discussed. One of the witnesses to provide testimony at the hearing was Dr. Lynton Caldwell.[8] An interchange during the hearing between Dr. Caldwell and Senator Jackson is considered by some as the point at which the provision behind the environmental impact statement requirement was introduced. Following are relevant excerpts from that testimony:

> Dr. Caldwell: I would urge that in shaping [an environmental] policy, it have an action-forcing, operational aspect ... For example, it seems that a statement of policy by the Congress should at least consider measures to require Federal agencies, in submitting proposals, to contain within the proposals an evaluation of the effect of those proposals upon the state of the environment...
>
> Senator Jackson: I have been concerned with the inadequacy of the policy declaration in the bill I have introduced. Obviously this is not enough. It does, however, provide a predicate from which to launch at a discussion as to what is required and how we should proceed ... [W]hat is needed in restructuring the governmental side of this problem is to legislatively create those situations that will bring about an action-forcing procedure the departments must comply with. Otherwise, these lofty declarations are nothing more than that.[9]

Senator Jackson further discussed the potential of broadening the policy provision in the bill to stipulate a general requirement applicable to all agencies that have responsibilities that affect the environment. In doing so, the Senator stated that he was "trying to avoid recodification of all the statutes."[10]

After the Senate hearing, Senator Jackson introduced amendments to the Senate bill.[11] Included in the amendments was a declaration of national environmental policy. Another amendment included a requirement that "all agencies of the Federal Government ... include in every recommendation or report on proposals for legislation and other major Federal actions significantly affecting the quality of the human environment, a *finding* by the responsible official that ... the environmental impact of the proposed action has been studied and considered."[12] [Emphasis added.]

In July 1969, the Senate passed its version of NEPA (S. 1075) without debate and no amendments offered. In September 1969, the House passed its version (H.R. 12549) by 372 to 15. The following December, the conference committee subsequently reported out a version containing various additions and compromises. In particular, in conference, the requirement for all major federal actions to be preceded by a "finding" on environmental impacts was changed to the requirement that a "detailed statement" on environmental impacts be prepared. The detailed statement would later be referred to as an environmental impact statement (EIS). Also included in conference was the requirement that certain federal agencies, other than the one preparing the EIS, be required to review the detailed statement.

It is unclear from the legislative history whether Congress intended for the EIS requirement to become the central element of NEPA compliance that it has. However, in addition to discussions regarding the need for action-forcing provisions to enforce the environmental policy, the legislative history includes statements regarding the need for federal agencies to consider the impacts of their actions. In discussing the relationship of the proposed legislation to existing policies and institutions, the Senate report states: "Many older operating agencies of the Federal Government ... do not at present have a mandate within the body of their enabling laws to allow them to give adequate attention to environmental values ... [The Senate bill] would provide all agencies and all Federal officials with a legislative mandate and a responsibility to consider the consequences of their actions on the environment."[13]

In late December, after minimal debate, both the House and Senate agreed to the conference report. On January 1, 1970, President Nixon signed NEPA into law.

In the more than 30 years since passage of NEPA, Congress has amended the law only to include minor technical changes.[14] However, within a year after NEPA's passage, a section was added to the Clean Air Act (42 U.S.C. 7401 et seq.) that affected the way NEPA is implemented. To further clarify agencies' responsibilities with regard to public involvement in the NEPA process, in December 1970, Congress added § 309 to the Clean Air Act.[15] Provisions of § 309 made explicit that the Administrator of the newly formed

Environmental Protection Agency (EPA) has a duty to examine and comment on all EISs. After that review, the Administrator was directed to make those comments public and, if the proposal was environmentally "unsatisfactory," to publish this finding and refer the matter to the CEQ. EPA subsequently developed a program for reviewing and rating federal agency projects (see "EPA's Unique Role in the NEPA Process" section, below).

## Overview of NEPA's Provisions

The goals of NEPA are to declare a national environmental policy, provide federal agencies with action-forcing provisions intended to ensure that the goals of the policy are implemented, establish the Council on Environmental Quality (CEQ) to provide advice to the President on environmental matters and to monitor the state of the environment, and require the President to submit to Congress an annual report on the state of the environment. These provisions are contained within NEPA's two titles. Title I declares a national environmental policy that states, in part:

> [I]t is the continuing policy of the Federal Government, in cooperation with State and local governments, and other concerned public and private organizations, to use all practicable means and measures ... to create and maintain conditions under which man and nature can exist in productive harmony ... [16]

The act also specifies broad national goals. NEPA declares that it is the "continuing responsibility of the Federal Government to use all practicable means, consistent with other essential considerations of national policy, to improve and coordinate Federal plans ... [so] that the Nation may—

- Fulfill the responsibilities of each generation as trustee of the environment for succeeding generations;
- Assure for all Americans safe, healthful, productive, and aesthetically and culturally pleasing surroundings;
- Attain the widest range of beneficial uses of the environment without degradation, risk to health or safety, or other undesirable and unintended consequences;

- Preserve important historic, cultural, and natural aspects of our national heritage, and maintain, wherever possible, an environment which supports diversity, and variety of individual choice;
- Achieve a balance between population and resource use which will permit high standards of living and a wide sharing of life's amenities; and
- Enhance the quality of renewable resources and approach the maximum attainable recycling of depletable resources."[17]

Title I also includes the action-forcing, procedural requirements intended to ensure that federal agencies adhere to NEPA's goals. Section 102 forms the basic framework for federal decision making under the "NEPA process." This section includes several provisions and requires that policies, regulations, and public laws of the United States be interpreted and administered according to NEPA's policies. Among other things, Section 102 requires federal agencies to use a "systematic, interdisciplinary approach" in planning and decision making that may have an impact on the environment.

To ensure that environmental impacts are considered, Section 102(2)(C) of NEPA requires all federal agencies to include in "every recommendation or report on proposals for legislation and other major Federal actions significantly affecting the quality of the human environment, a detailed statement by the responsible official on the environmental impact of the proposed action."[18] In addition to environmental impacts, federal agencies are required to provide an analysis of

- any adverse environmental effects that cannot be avoided should the proposal be implemented,
- alternatives to the proposed action,
- the relationship between local short-term uses of man's environment and the maintenance and enhancement of long-term productivity, and
- any irreversible and irretrievable commitments of resources that would be involved in the proposed action should it be implemented.[19]

NEPA also requires federal agencies to study and develop appropriate alternatives to the recommended action for any project involving "unresolved conflicts concerning alternative uses of available resources."[20] This requirement is not limited to actions that require an environmental impact statement.

Section 103 of NEPA directs all federal agencies to review their existing statutory authority, administrative regulations, and policies and procedures to determine whether any deficiencies or inconsistencies would "prohibit full compliance with the purposes and provisions" of the act.[21] After conducting this review, the agencies are directed to take necessary measures to make their policies conform with NEPA's intent. NEPA also states that its policies and goals are supplementary to existing law.[22]

Title II of NEPA establishes the CEQ in the Executive Office of the President and specifies its responsibilities. It requires CEQ to submit to Congress an annual Environmental Quality Report on such topics as the condition of the environment, trends in the quality of the environment, and a review of federal, state and local programs to address environmental concerns.[23] Also, the act specifies a list of duties and functions that allow CEQ to support the President in information gathering and policy making with regard to environmental issues.

## The Evolution of NEPA's Implementation

NEPA is a declaration of policy with action-forcing provisions, not a regulatory statute comparable to other environmental laws intended to protect air, water, wetlands, or endangered species.[24] It establishes the basic framework for integrating environmental considerations into federal decision making. However, the law itself does not provide details on how this process should be accomplished.

With an initial absence of regulations specifying implementation procedures and no agency authorized to enforce its requirements, federal agencies have reacted in different ways to NEPA's requirements. Some initially had difficulty complying with NEPA. Others believed that they were not required to comply with NEPA's provisions at all. As a result, litigation to enforce agency compliance with NEPA's mandate began almost immediately.

In addition to questions of procedure (e.g., how, when, or why an EIS must be prepared), another question ultimately to be determined was how the environmental policy goals of the act should be implemented or enforced. The courts and CEQ played significant roles in determining how those questions were answered and, consequently, how NEPA was ultimately implemented.

## The Role of the Courts in Implementing NEPA

Almost since NEPA's enactment, the courts have played a prominent role in interpreting and, in effect, enforcing NEPA's requirements.[25] Beginning almost immediately and continuing into the early 1980s, the courts emphasized agency compliance with NEPA's procedural EIS requirements but did little to delineate specific compliance requirements connected to the substantive environmental policy goals. In 1983, the U.S. Supreme Court clarified that

> NEPA has twin aims. First, it places upon an agency the obligation to consider every significant aspect of the environmental impact of a proposed action. Second, it ensures that the agency will inform the public that it has indeed considered environmental concerns in its decision making process. Congress in enacting NEPA, however, did not require agencies to elevate environmental concerns over other appropriate considerations. Rather, it required only that the agency take a "hard look" at the environmental consequences before taking a major action ... Congress did not enact NEPA, of course, so that an agency would contemplate the environmental impact of an action as an abstract exercise. Rather, Congress intended that the "hard look" be incorporated as part of the agency's process of deciding whether to pursue a particular federal action.[26]

This specification of NEPA's "twin aims" and the "hard look" requirement are often cited by both federal agencies and environmental advocates to articulate NEPA's mandate. In 1989, the U.S. Supreme Court reiterated that NEPA does not mandate particular results, but simply prescribes a process.[27] If the adverse environmental effects of a proposed action are adequately identified and evaluated, NEPA does not constrain an agency from deciding that other values outweigh the environmental costs. The Court further clarified that "other statutes may impose substantive environmental obligations on federal agencies, but NEPA merely prohibits uninformed, rather than unwise, agency action."[28]

In addition to determining the substantive versus procedural question, the courts have determined many specific procedural elements of NEPA compliance. For example, for individual actions, courts have ruled on agency interpretation of the meaning of the phrases "federal action," "significantly affecting," and "human environment." Also, the courts played a significant role in determining how and when federal agencies were required to prepare EISs. Some questions decided by the courts involved such issues as the adequacy of individual EISs, who must prepare an EIS, at what point an EIS must be prepared, and how adverse comments from agencies should be handled. Such decisions were, at least in part, the basis of CEQ guidelines released during the 1970s and were subsequently considered when CEQ promulgated its regulations (see "The Role of CEQ in Implementing NEPA" section, below).

The role of the courts in implementing the NEPA process has sometimes been controversial. Critics of NEPA charge that opponents of a given federal project will use litigation related to the NEPA process to delay or halt a project. Others assert that litigation is used primarily when an agency does not comply with its own NEPA procedures (see "NEPA Implementation and Project Delays" section, below).

## The Role of CEQ in Implementing NEPA

Authority to promulgate regulations to implement NEPA's provisions was not expressly included among the duties and responsibilities given to CEQ under NEPA. However, shortly after signing NEPA, President Nixon issued an Executive Order authorizing CEQ to issue "regulations" for the implementation of the procedural provisions of the act.[29] The Executive Order directed CEQ to develop regulations that would be

> [D]esigned to make the environmental impact statement process more useful to decision makers and the public; and to reduce paperwork and the accumulation of extraneous background data, in order to emphasize the need to focus on real environmental issues and alternatives ... [and] require impact statements to be concise, clear, and to the point, and supported by evidence that agencies have made the necessary environmental analyses.

The Executive Order also directed federal agencies to hold public meetings and promote public involvement in the NEPA process. The Executive Order did not extend to CEQ the authority to make these regulations legally binding on federal agencies. Therefore, they would serve as only guidance for compliance.

During the 1970s, CEQ continued to issue guidelines that addressed the basic requirements of EIS preparation. CEQ left NEPA implementation largely to the discretion of federal agencies, which were to use the CEQ guidelines to prepare their own procedures. Still, many agencies were slow to do so, with many initially arguing that NEPA did not apply to them.[30]

During the mid-1970s, frequent complaints were raised regarding the delays that the NEPA process was perceived to cause in the decision-making process. Some observers attributed these problems to a lack of uniformity in NEPA implementation and uncertainty regarding what was required of federal agencies.[31] Also, in response to increasing NEPA-related litigation, agencies often produced overly lengthy, unreadable, and unused EISs.[32] In an effort to standardize an increasingly complicated NEPA process, President Carter amended President Nixon's Executive Order, directing CEQ to issue regulations that would be legally binding on federal agencies.[33] Final regulations replacing the previous guidelines were issued in the fall of 1978 and became effective on July 30, 1979.[34] CEQ's regulations were intended to foster better decision making and reduce the paperwork and delays associated with NEPA compliance.[35] CEQ's regulations also specified that the purpose of the NEPA process was to

- inform federal agencies of what they must do to comply with the procedures and achieve the goals of NEPA;
- ensure that the environmental information made available to public officials and citizens is of high quality (i.e., includes accurate scientific analysis, expert agency comments, and public scrutiny);
- foster better decision making by helping public officials make decisions based on an understanding of the environmental consequences of their actions; and
- facilitate public involvement in the federal decision-making process.[36]

CEQ's regulations, drawn in large part from its guidelines, included several noteworthy clarifications and amplifications to requirements specified in the law. For example, the regulations

- required agencies to include a project-"scoping" process to identify important environmental issues and related review requirements before writing the EIS;
- required EISs to be prepared in multiple stages (draft and final), with supplemental EISs required under specific circumstances;
- provided criteria for determining the significance of impacts and what constituted a "major federal action";

- defined and specified the roles of "lead agencies" (those responsible for preparing the NEPA documentation) and "cooperating agencies" (agencies that participate in or contribute to the preparation of the NEPA documentation);
- allowed lead agencies to set time limits on milestones in the NEPA process and page limits on documentation;
- specified a dispute resolution process between lead agencies and EPA (required originally under § 309 of the Clean Air Act), if EPA determined the EIS to be "unsatisfactory";
- specified environmental review procedures and documents applicable to projects that had uncertain or insignificant environmental impacts;
- specified how an agency was to involve the public in the NEPA process;
- required, for actions involving an EIS, that a public record of decision be published when a final agency decision is made; and
- provided for alternative compliance procedures in the event of an emergency.

The CEQ regulations were intended to be generic in nature. Each federal agency was required to develop its own NEPA procedures that would be specific to typical classes of actions undertaken by that agency.[37] Separately, CEQ regulations directed federal agencies to review their existing policies, procedures, and regulations to ensure that they were in full compliance with the intent of NEPA.[38]

CEQ's regulations are unique in several aspects. For example, they were issued eight years after enactment of the law they implement. As a result, they reflect not only CEQ's interpretation of NEPA, but also the initial interpretation of the courts and the administrative experiences of other agencies. Also, the CEQ regulations incorporated provisions of another law—§ 309 of the Clean Air Act (i.e., procedures for referring projects to CEQ for dispute resolution when EPA has found them to be environmentally unsatisfactory). Finally, although CEQ has oversight of the implementation of its regulations, it is not authorized to *enforce* them.

In addition to promulgating regulations in 1978, CEQ has provided support and informal guidance to federal agencies implementing NEPA's requirements.[39] For example, in 1981, CEQ issued its "Forty Most Asked Questions Concerning CEQ's NEPA Regulations." Answers to those questions deal with topics such as how to determine the range of alternatives considered in an EIS, how environmental documents should be made public, and the scope of mitigation measures required to be discussed. Also, in 2010, after NEPA's $40^{th}$ birthday, CEQ proposed guidance intended to "Modernize and Reinvigorate NEPA."[40] Included was draft guidance for public comment on when and how federal agencies must consider greenhouse gas emissions and climate change in their proposed actions. CEQ had been asked to provide guidance on this subject informally by federal agencies and formally by a petition under the Administrative Procedure Act. The draft guidance was intended to explain how federal agencies should analyze the environmental impacts of greenhouse gas emissions and climate change when they describe the environmental impacts of a proposed action under NEPA.

## DETERMINING WHEN NEPA APPLIES

Under NEPA, an environmental impact statement must be prepared for "every recommendation or report on proposals for legislation and other major federal actions significantly affecting the quality of the human environment." Interpretation of each element of this phrase has been the subject of myriad court decisions and guidance from CEQ. Two terms of particular relevance are "federal action" and "significantly." In determining whether and how NEPA will apply to an action, it is necessary to determine whether an action is in fact a federal one and, if so, whether its environmental impacts will be significant.

### Federal Actions Subject to NEPA

To determine whether NEPA applies to an action, it is first necessary to determine whether it is a federal one.[41] "Federal" actions include those that are potentially subject to federal control and responsibility. Such actions include "projects and programs entirely or partly funded, assisted, conducted, regulated, or approved by federal agencies."[42] Specifically, federal agency compliance with NEPA may be required for actions that require a federal permit or other regulatory decision to proceed.[43]

In many cases, it is immediately apparent that a project or program is federal (as opposed to a strictly private or state action[44]). However, in some instances, such as private actions in which a federal agency has some small involvement, a determination is not as clear.[45] CEQ regulations specify categories of actions within which NEPA-covered federal actions tend to fall (see Table 1).

**Table 1. Typical Categories of "Federal Actions" Subject to NEPA**

| Category of action | Examples |
|---|---|
| Site-specific projects | Construction or management activities located in a defined geographic area; actions requiring federal licensing, permitting, or other regulatory decision; activity requiring federal assistance or funding. |
| Adoption of programs | Projects that may include groups of concerted actions to implement a specific policy or plan; systematic and connected agency decisions allocating agency resources to implement a specific statutory program or executive directive. |
| Adoption of plans | May include official documents prepared or approved by federal agencies which guide or prescribe alternative uses of federal resources, upon which future agency actions will be based (agencies may argue that certain plans do not fit the definition of an "action" in accordance with NEPA). |
| Adoption of policy | May include the adoption of official policy, such as rules, regulations, and interpretations adopted pursuant to the Administrative Procedure Act (5 U.S.C. § 551 et seq.); treaties and international conventions or agreements (also, Executive Order 12114, Environmental Effects Abroad of Major Federal Actions, specifies environmental review requirements for actions taken outside the United States); or formal documents establishing an agency's policies that will result in or substantially alter agency programs. |

Source: 40 C.F.R. § 1508.18(b).

A broad NEPA review may be done for the adoption of programs, plans, or policies. Such a review would most likely be followed by a site-specific review for any subsequently implemented projects. This process of producing a broad statement, followed by a more narrowly focused NEPA analysis is referred to as "tiering."[46] In such a project, the NEPA documentation need only summarize the issues discussed in the broader document and incorporate previous discussions by reference. Such a process is recommended to avoid repetitive discussion of the same issues. See http://www.serconline.org/SEQA/stateactivity.html.

Table 2 lists examples of projects at selected agencies that may fall into one of the categories of actions that require environmental review under NEPA.

**Table 2. Selected Examples of Agency Actions Requiring Environmental Review Under NEPA**

| Agency | Project types |
|---|---|
| Department of Agriculture | Forest Service—Private timber, grazing, or mining operations on Forest Service land. |
| Department of Defense | Army Corps of Engineers—Flood control projects, ecosystem restoration projects, water resources projects, or projects requiring a federal permit for dredge and fill operations. |
| Department of Energy | Approval of dam construction, the process of siting of oil and gas pipelines on federal land, the process of siting power transmission lines on federal land, and research operations. |
| Department of Housing and Urban Development | Construction of affordable housing projects; certain projects that would remove, demolish, convert, or substantially rehabilitate existing housing units; or the extension of urban development grants or block grant programs. |
| Department of the Interior | Bureau of Land Management—Private mining operations on federal land; and oil and gas drilling operations on federal lands. |
| Department of Transportation | Federal Highway Administration—Highway and bridge construction, maintenance, and repair. |
| | Federal Aviation Administration—Airport construction and expansion. |
| EPA | Issuance of permits under the National Pollutant Discharge Elimination System (NPDES). |

Source: Congressional Research Service (CRS) review of individual agency actions.

Although such application is rare, NEPA also is intended to apply to agency proposals for federal legislation. CEQ's definition of legislation includes "a bill or legislative proposal to Congress developed by or with the significant cooperation and support of a Federal agency.... "[47] This definition does not include requests for appropriations. The test for "significant cooperation" is whether the proposal is predominantly that of the agency rather than another source. Only the agency with primary responsibility for the subject matter involved is required to prepare a legislative EIS.

## Determining the Significance of a Federal Action

The requirement to prepare an EIS depends on whether the federal action will have impacts "significantly affecting the quality of the human environment." In the years after NEPA was enacted, a question that was often disputed between federal agencies and third parties, and ultimately decided by the courts, was whether a given federal action had a "significant" impact. Most federal actions have *some* impact on the environment. Determining the degree of impact is necessary to determine how to comply with NEPA's procedural requirements.

CEQ regulations do not list specific types of projects that have significant environmental impacts or definitively define "significantly." Instead, the regulations require agencies to determine the significance of a project's impacts on a case-by-case basis, based on its context and intensity.[48]

Determining the context of a project involves analyzing the significance of its impacts to society as a whole, an affected region, affected interests, or the locality.[49] A site-specific project may require analysis of the local significance of the project, whereas a programmatic action may have nationwide significance. The degree of significance may depend on factors such as the location and scope of the project. For example, the impacts of a site-specific project on 1 acre of a 2,000- acre wetland may be insignificant compared with a project that affects 1 acre of a 2-acre wetland.

Intensity refers to the severity of a project's impacts. Factors used to assess an impact's intensity must be determined on a case-by-case basis. However, CEQ specifies the following minimum factors that must be evaluated:

- Environmental impacts that may be beneficial *and* adverse.
- The degree to which the proposed action affects public health or safety.
- Unique characteristics of the geographical area, such as proximity to historic or cultural resources, park lands, prime farmlands, wetlands, wild and scenic rivers, or ecologically critical areas.
- The degree to which the effects on the quality of the human environment are likely to be highly controversial (in this context,

"controversy" relates only to the interpretation of the environmental effects of a project—not to the potential controversy or unpopularity of the project as a whole).

- The degree to which the possible effects on the human environment are highly uncertain or involve unique or unknown risks.
- The degree to which the action may establish a precedent for future actions with significant effects.
- Whether the action is related to other actions with individually insignificant but cumulatively significant impacts.
- The degree to which the action may adversely affect resources listed in, or eligible for, the National Register of Historic Places or may cause loss or destruction of significant scientific, cultural, or historical resources.
- The degree to which the action may adversely affect an endangered or threatened species or its habitat.
- Whether the action threatens a violation of federal, state, or local law or requirements imposed for the protection of the environment.[50]

Individual agencies may consider additional factors based on environmental impacts common to the types of projects pursued by that agency. Further, to adequately determine an impact's intensity, input from other agencies may be needed. For example, if a highway will cut across prime farmland, the Department of Transportation (DOT) may need assistance from the U.S. Department of Agriculture (USDA) to determine the intensity of the project's impacts.

Because degrees of impact must be evaluated to determine project significance, such an evaluation may require subjective judgments. Therefore, a clear administrative record is generally considered necessary to demonstrate that an agency appropriately determined the significance of a project's impacts.

## OVERVIEW OF THE NEPA PROCESS

The NEPA process includes the steps a federal agency must take to document that consideration was given to determine the significance of a proposed action's environmental impacts. For some actions, it may not be readily apparent that environmental impacts will be significant. Some projects clearly have little or no significant impact, but they still require an agency to demonstrate that the level of impacts was considered. To account for this variability, CEQ regulations establish the following three classes of action, which determine how compliance with NEPA analysis is documented:

- Actions Requiring an EIS—When it is *known* that the action will have a significant environmental impact.
- Actions Requiring an Environmental Assessment (EA)—When the significance of environmental impacts is *uncertain* and must be determined.
- Actions that are Categorically Excluded—Those which normally do not individually or cumulatively have a significant effect on the human environment.

The requirement to produce an EIS is probably the most familiar element of NEPA compliance. However, actions requiring an EIS account for a small percentage of all federal actions proposed in a given year. For example, in 2008, 543 EISs were filed with EPA (this total includes draft, final, and supplemental EISs).[51] CEQ estimates that the vast majority of federal actions require an EA or are categorically excluded from the requirement to prepare an EA or EIS.

Determining the total number of federal actions subject to NEPA is difficult, as most agencies track only the number of actions requiring an EIS. Also, as indicated in the figures above, agencies track the total draft, final, and supplemental EISs filed in a given year, not the total number of individual federal actions requiring an EIS in a given year. One agency that does track all projects is DOT's Federal Highway Administration (FHWA). According to FHWA, in 2007, approximately 4% of all highway projects required an EIS, 4% required an EA, and almost 92% were classified as categorically excluded. Although projects requiring an EIS or EA represent a relatively low percentage of all projects, those projects represented a comparatively large percentage of total FHWA funding. For example, while projects requiring an EIS or EA represented 8% of the total number of projects, they accounted for almost 23% of the funds allocated by FHWA in 2007. Projects classified as categorical exclusions accounted for almost 77% of FHWA funds.[52]

## Environmental Impact Statements

As soon as practicable after its decision to prepare an EIS, the agency preparing it (the "lead agency") is required to publish a notice of intent (NOI) in the *Federal Register*.[53] The NOI acts as the formal announcement of the project to the public and to interested federal, state, tribal, and local agencies.

As soon as possible after, or in conjunction with, the determination that an EIS is needed, the agency is required to determine the scope of the project. During the scoping process the "lead agency" must

- identify and invite the participation of affected parties, including federal, state, or local agencies or Indian tribes; proponents of the actions; and other interested persons;
- identify significant issues to be analyzed in depth in the EIS;
- identify and eliminate issues that are *not* significant or have been covered by prior environmental review from detailed study;
- allocate assignments for preparing the EIS to relevant agencies; and
- identify other environmental review and consultation requirements so that analyses and studies required other under federal, state, local or tribal laws may be prepared concurrently, rather than sequentially, with the EIS.[54]

During the scoping process, the lead agency may set time and page limits for an individual EIS. The agency should also determine any environmental laws, regulations, or executive orders, in addition to NEPA, that may apply to the project. For example, the agency should determine in the scoping process whether the project may affect property of historical significance, endangered species habitat, or wetlands or navigable waters—each of which may require compliance with the National Historic Preservation Act, the Endangered Species Act, or the Clean Water Act, respectively.

Once the scope of the action has been determined, EIS preparation can begin. Preparation is done in two stages, resulting in a draft and a final EIS.[55] The draft EIS should be prepared in accordance with the scope of the project and, to the fullest extent possible, meet requirements of § 102(2)(C) of NEPA. The final EIS should respond to any participating agency comments and address any inadequacies in the draft EIS. A supplemental EIS may be required in some instances. A summary of the components of an EIS, as required under CEQ's regulations, is provided in Table 3.

**Table 3. Components of an EIS**

| EIS Component | Description |
|---|---|
| Purpose and Need Statement | A brief statement, developed by the lead agency, specifying the underlying purpose of a project and the need to which the agency is responding (40 C.F.R. § 1502.13). |
| Alternatives | A discussion of the range of alternatives, including the proposed action, that will meet the project's purpose and need. The discussion should explore and objectively evaluate all "reasonable" alternatives, and for alternatives which were eliminated from detailed study, a brief discussion of the reasons for their having been eliminated. A "no action" alternative may also be required to establish a baseline against which other alternatives may be compared (40 C.F.R. § 1502.14). |
| Affected Environment | A succinct description of the environment of the area(s) to be affected by the alternatives under consideration. For example, the affected environment may include wetlands, prime farmland, urban areas, historic sites, or endangered species habitat (40 C.F.R. § 1502.15). |
| Environmental Consequences | An analysis of impacts of each alternative on the affected environment, including a discussion of the probable beneficial and adverse social, economic, and environmental effects of each alternative. This section must also include, where applicable, a discussion of both the direct and indirect effects of each alternative and the significance of those effects; a description of the measures proposed to mitigate adverse impacts; and methods of compliance with any applicable legal requirements may (e.g., whether and how compliance with the Endangered Species Act will be accomplished if endangered species habitat is impacted) (40 C.F.R. § 1502.16). |
| List of Preparers | List of names and qualifications of individuals responsible for preparing the EIS (40 C.F.R. § 1502.17). |
| Appendix | Any material prepared in connection with the EIS. Such materials normally consist of material which substantiates any analysis fundamental to the EIS (40 C.F.R. § 1502.18). |

Source: CRS review of requirements in 40 C.F.R. § 1502.

The action's purpose and need statement is the foundation on which subsequent sections of the EIS are built. No hard-and-fast regulatory definition of "purpose and need" exists. However, as it has been interpreted, the statement cannot be so narrow that it effectively defines competing "reasonable alternatives" out of consideration. The "purpose" of an action may be a discussion of the goals and objective of an action. The "need" may be a discussion of existing conditions that call for some improvement.

The goals defined in the purpose and need evaluation facilitate the development of viable project alternatives. CEQ regulations refer to the alternatives section of the EIS as the "heart" of the document.[56] Alternatives that must be considered include those that are practical and feasible from a technical, economic, and common-sense standpoint, rather than simply desirable from the standpoint of the agency or a potentially affected stakeholder.[57] Large, complex projects may have a large number of reasonable alternatives. In this case, CEQ suggests that only a representative number of the most reasonable examples, covering the full range of alternatives, should be presented.[58]

Once the final EIS is approved and the agency decides to take action, the lead agency must prepare a public record of decision (ROD). CEQ regulations specify that the ROD must include a statement of the final decision, all alternatives considered by the agency in reaching its decision, and whether all practicable means to avoid or minimize environmental harm from the selected alternative have been adopted and, if not, why they were not.[59]

Generally, once the ROD has been issued, an agency's action may proceed (as long as other statutory requirements are met). In addition to the EIS and the ROD, the final procedural record of the NEPA process may include, but is not limited to, planning documents, notices, scoping hearings, documents supporting findings in the EIS, public comments, and agency responses.[60]

## Environmental Assessments

If an agency is uncertain whether an action's impacts on the environment will be significant, it usually prepares an environmental assessment (EA). An EA is carried out to clarify issues and determine the extent of an action's environmental effects. CEQ regulations define an EA as a concise public document that (1) provides sufficient evidence and analysis for determining whether to prepare an EIS or a finding of no significant impact (FONSI), (2) aids agency compliance with NEPA when no EIS is required, and (3) facilitates preparation of an EIS when one is necessary.[61]

The CEQ regulations require no standard format for EAs; however, the regulations do require agencies to include a brief discussion of the need for the proposal, alternatives, impacts of the proposal and alternatives, and a list of agencies and individuals consulted.[62] Individual agency regulations and guidance may include more specific requirements. Some agencies suggest that the process for developing an EA should be similar to developing an EIS. For example, the applicant should consult interested agencies to scope the project to determine the potential for social, economic, or environmental impacts; briefly discuss the project's purpose and need; identify project alternatives and measures to mitigate adverse impacts; and identify any other environmental review requirements applicable to the project (e.g., permitting requirements under Section 404 of the Clean Water Act). Public participation in the EA process is left largely to the discretion of the lead agency.

If at any time during preparation of the EA, a project's impacts are determined to be significant, EIS preparation should begin. If the impacts are determined not to be significant, the lead agency must prepare a FONSI. The FONSI serves as the agency's administrative record in support of its decision regarding a project's impact. The FONSI also must be available to the public.[63]

## Categorical Exclusions

If a project is of a type or in a category known to have no significant environmental impacts, it is categorically excluded from the requirement to prepare and EA or EIS. Individual agencies are required to specifically list, in their respective NEPA regulations, those projects that are likely to be considered categorical exclusions (CEs).[64] For example, DOT has identified the construction of bicycle and pedestrian lanes, landscaping, and the installation of traffic signals as actions that would generally be classified as categorical exclusions.[65]

Whether or what types of documentation may be required to demonstrate that a project is categorically excluded will depend on whether the project involves extraordinary circumstances that may cause a normally excluded action to have a significant environmental effect.[66] An individual agency's NEPA requirements may specify criteria under which otherwise excluded actions may require documentation to prove that the CE determination is appropriate.

Although categorically excluded projects do not have significant environmental impacts, an agency may require a certain level of documentation to prove that the CE determination is appropriate. Also, the fact that a project does not have a significant impact, as defined under NEPA, does not mean that it will not trigger statutory requirements of other environmental laws. For example, if historical sites, endangered species habitats, wetlands, or properties in minority neighborhoods, to name a few, are affected by a proposed federal action, compliance with related environmental laws, in addition to NEPA, may be required.

In 2010, CEQ released "Guidance Clarifying Use of Categorical Exclusions."[67] This guidance was designed to ensure that agencies establish and use categorical exclusions appropriately and transparently. It also calls on agencies to review their existing categorical exclusions periodically to avoid the use of outdated NEPA procedures.

# AGENCY PARTICIPATION IN THE NEPA PROCESS

Federal actions to which NEPA applies involve the participation of a "lead agency" and "cooperating agencies." As stated previously, the lead agency is the federal agency that takes responsibility for preparing the NEPA documentation.[68] State or local agencies may act, with the federal lead agency, as joint lead agencies. The project applicant[69] may initially develop substantive portions of the environmental document; however, the lead agency is responsible for its scope and overall content. A cooperating agency is any federal agency, other than a lead agency, that has jurisdiction by law or special expertise regarding any environmental impact involved in a proposal.[70] A tribal, state, or local agency may also be a cooperating agency. Table 4 lists selected statutes that may apply to a given federal action and the corresponding agency that could subsequently be required to participate in the NEPA process.

## Responsibilities of the Lead and Cooperating Agencies

At the request of the lead agency, the cooperating agency is required to assume responsibility for developing information and preparing environmental analyses, including portions of the EIS related to its special expertise. Such a role may be set out in a memorandum of understanding or agreement between the agencies. A cooperating agency may be excused from some or all of these responsibilities if precluded by other program requirements.

**Table 4. Selected Federal Statutes and Potential Corresponding Key Cooperating Agencies**

| Statute | Potential cooperating agency |
|---|---|
| National Historic Preservation Act | Advisory Council on Historic Preservation and/or state or tribal historic preservation officer |
| Endangered Species Act | The Department of the Interior's U.S. Fish and Wildlife Service and/or the Department of Commerce's National Marine Fisheries Service |
| Clean Water Act | The Army Corps of Engineers and/or EPA |
| Wild and Scenic Rivers Act | The agency responsible for managing the listed or study river (e.g., the National Park Service, U.S. Fish and Wildlife Service, Bureau of Land Management, or Forest Service) |
| Statute | Potential cooperating agency |
| Farmland Protection Policy Act | The Natural Resources Conservation Service of USDA |

Source: Table prepared by CR and based on the likely applicability of selected federal statutes.

Note: Tribal, state, and local agencies may also be included among those required to participate in a given EIS.

Some projects have involved disagreements regarding the authority of and extent to which coordinating agencies should be involved in the NEPA process. For example, some stakeholders have expressed confusion regarding the degree to which a coordinating agency has the right to influence the development of certain elements of an EIS. In 2003, this issue of agency authority was the subject of correspondence between Transportation Secretary Norman Mineta and CEQ Chairman James Connaughton. Secretary Mineta asked for clarification regarding the role of lead and cooperating agencies with regard to developing purpose and need statements.[71] Secretary Mineta referred to the sometimes extended interagency debates over purpose and need statements as a cause of delay in highway project development. In his response, Chairman Connaughton referred to CEQ regulations specifying that the lead agency has the authority and responsibility to define a project's purpose and need. Further, Chairman Connaughton referenced previous federal court decisions giving deference to the lead agency in determining a project's purpose and need. Chairman Connaughton's letter also quotes CEQ's regulations, citing the lead agency's "responsibilities throughout the NEPA process for the 'scope, objectivity, and content of the entire statement or of any other responsibility' under NEPA."

## Addressing Agency Comments

Before completing an EIS, the lead agency is required to consult with and obtain comments from cooperating agencies regarding any environmental impact involved in the proposed action.[72] The CEQ regulations specify requirements for inviting and responding to comments on the draft EIS.[73] In addition to the cooperating agencies, which must comment, the lead agency is required to request comments from appropriate state, local, or tribal agencies; the public, particularly those persons or organizations who may be interested in or affected by the action (see further discussion under the "Demonstrating Public Involvement" section, below); any agency that has requested to receive EISs on similar actions; and the applicant (if there is one).[74]

If a lead agency receives comments on a NEPA document, the agency is required to assess and consider those comments and respond in one or more of the following ways:

- Modify proposed alternatives, including the proposed action.
- Develop and evaluate alternatives not previously considered.
- Supplement, improve, or modify its analyses.
- Make factual corrections in the EIS.
- Explain why the comments do not warrant further response from the lead agency, citing the sources, authorities, or reasons that support the agency's position and, if appropriate, indicate circumstances that would trigger agency reappraisal or further response.[75]

Under CEQ regulations, lead agencies are required to invite comments on a draft EIS, cooperating agencies have a duty to comment on it, and lead agencies are required to respond to those comments. As illustrated in the choices listed above, the lead agency is not precluded from moving forward with a project if it sufficiently addresses those comments. However, if negative comments are received, to avoid a potential legal challenge after the project has reached an advanced stage of development, the lead agency is well-served to resolve the issue.

### EPA's Unique Role in the NEPA Process

Independent of its potential to participate as a lead or cooperating agency,[76] EPA has two distinct roles in the NEPA process. The first regards its duty, under § 309 of the Clean Air Act, to review and comment publicly on the environmental impacts of proposed federal activities, including those for which an EIS is prepared.

After conducting its review, EPA must rate the adequacy of the EIS and the environmental impact of the action.[77] The EIS may be rated "adequate," "needs more information," or "inadequate." The lead agency is required to respond appropriately, depending on EPA's rating. With regard to rating the environmental impacts of an action, EPA would rate a project in one of the following four ways: lack of objections, environmental concerns, environmental objections, or environmentally unsatisfactory. If it determines that the action is environmentally unsatisfactory, EPA is required to refer the matter to CEQ for dispute resolution.[78] However, such referral should be made only after concerted, timely, but unsuccessful attempts to resolve differences with the lead agency.[79]

EPA's second duty is an administrative one, in which it carries out the operational duties associated with the EIS filing process. In 1978, these duties were transferred to EPA by CEQ in accordance with terms of a Memorandum of Agreement (MOA).[80] Under the MOA, EPA's Office of Federal Activities is designated the official recipient of all EISs prepared by federal agencies. EPA maintains a national EIS filing system. By maintaining the system, EPA facilitates public access to EISs by publishing weekly notices in the *Federal Register* of EISs available for public review, along with summaries of EPA's comments.

## DEMONSTRATING PUBLIC INVOLVEMENT

As the law has been interpreted, one of the primary goals of NEPA is to give the public a meaningful opportunity to learn about and comment on the proposed actions of the federal government *before* decisions are made and actions are taken. To meet this goal, CEQ's regulations require agencies to encourage and facilitate public involvement in decisions that significantly affect the quality of the human environment (i.e., projects that require an EIS).[81]

Specifically, agencies are required to provide public notice of NEPA-related hearings, public meetings, and the availability of environmental documents so as to inform public stakeholders that may be interested in or affected by a proposed action.[82] Documentation related to the public's participation in the NEPA process (e.g., public comments or hearings transcripts) must be included in the final EIS.

As mentioned above, the lead agency must seek and respond to public comments. Public stakeholders likely to comment on federal actions will vary according to the action. They may include individuals or groups expected to benefit from or be adversely affected by the project, or special interest groups with concerns about the project's environmental impacts. For example, a road-widening project may have an impact on adjacent homes or businesses. Such a project may elicit comments from the local business community (e.g., individual businesses, the Chamber of Commerce, or local development organizations) and area home owners. A project with impacts on sensitive environmental resources, such as wetlands or endangered species, may generate comments from environmental interest groups.

If stakeholders have concerns about a project's impacts, their comments may be directed at virtually any element of that project, the NEPA process, or related documentation. If stakeholder comments are not addressed sufficiently, stakeholders may respond by filing suit.

To avoid conflict after a project has reached an advanced stage of development, CEQ recommends that continuous contact with nonagency stakeholders be maintained throughout the decision-making process—from the earliest project planning stages to the selection of a particular alternative, including the intervening stages to define purpose and need and to develop a range of potential alternatives. The need for such contact was illustrated in a 1997 CEQ study.

Study results found that one element of the NEPA process critical to effective and efficient implementation was "... the extent to which an agency takes into account the views of the surrounding community and other interested members of the public during its planning and decision making process."[83]

CEQ regulations specify public involvement requirements only for federal actions requiring an EIS. Agencies may devise their own policy regarding public involvement in the preparation of an EA or in making a categorical exclusion determination.

## THE USE OF NEPA AS AN ' ' UMBRELLA' ' STATUTE

Large, complex actions, such as bridge and highway construction, mining operations, or oil and gas development on public lands, may require compliance with literally dozens of federal, state, tribal, and local laws. Depending on the resources present at a project site, compliance with various categories of legal requirements may apply to a given federal action, as illustrated in Table 5.

**Table 5. Categories of Legal Requirements Potentially Applicable to Federal Actions**

| Category of laws | Selected potential corresponding authorities |
|---|---|
| Laws intended to protect physical resources | Clean Air Act |
| | Clean Water Act |
| | Pollution Prevention Act |
| | Safe Drinking Water Act |
| Laws intended to protect cultural resources | National Historic Preservation Act |
| | Archaeological and Historical Preservation Act |
| | Historic Sites and Buildings Act |
| Laws intended to protect natural resources | Endangered Species Act |
| | Marine Mammal Protection Act |
| | Fish and Wildlife Coordination Act |
| | Migratory Bird Treaty Act |
| Laws intended to minimize impacts to communities or individuals | Emergency Planning and Community Right to Know Act |
| | Farmland Protection Policy Act |
| | Title VI of the Civil Rights Act |
| Special status land use laws | Wild and Scenic Rivers Act |
| | The Coastal Zone Management Act |
| | Wilderness Act |

Source: Table prepared by CRS and based on a review of selected federal actions.
Note: Tribal, state, or local laws may also be applicable to a given impacted resource.

To integrate the compliance process and avoid duplication of effort, NEPA regulations specify that, to the fullest extent possible, agencies must prepare the EIS concurrently with *any* environmental requirements.[84] The EIS must list any federal permits, licenses, and other entitlements required to implement the proposed project. In this capacity, NEPA functions as an "umbrella" statute; any study, review, or consultation required by any other law that is related to the environment should be conducted within the framework of the NEPA process.

NEPA forms the framework to coordinate and demonstrate compliance with these requirements. NEPA itself does not *require* compliance with them. Theoretically, if the requirement to comply with NEPA were removed, compliance with each applicable law would still be required. The use of NEPA as an umbrella statute can lead to confusion in this regard. For example, consider a project alternative that requires compliance with the Endangered Species Act (ESA). One required element of the EIS may include a demonstration that, among other potential requirements, a biological assessment be prepared in compliance with the ESA. The requirement to comply with the ESA, including the involvement of the appropriate agency with jurisdiction over compliance, would simply be *identified* within the framework of the NEPA process, not required by NEPA.

## NEPA Implementation and Project Delays

Stakeholders such as state and local project sponsors and industry representatives with an interest in the implementation of a federal action sometimes charge that NEPA implementation is inefficient and overly time-consuming, leading to what they perceive as unnecessary delays in needed government actions. Some agency representatives feel that the NEPA process, when implemented as required by the CEQ regulations, actually facilitates a more efficiently executed project. Environmental organizations look at the NEPA process as a necessary step in ensuring that the public gets a voice in the federal decision-making process and that expediting that process is not necessarily in the best interest of the public or the environment. Further, they argue that blaming the environmental compliance process for project delays is misplaced. One argument is that federal projects may be delayed because resource agencies, required by law to participate in the compliance process, are overburdened and not sufficiently funded, staffed, or equipped to meet the demand.

## Causes of Project Delays Attributed to the NEPA Process

Delays attributed to the NEPA process fall into two broad categories—those related to the time it takes to complete required documentation and delays resulting from NEPA-related litigation.

In the past, particularly in the years after NEPA was implemented, the preparation of NEPA documentation played a role in delaying individual federal actions. However, there is little data available to demonstrate that NEPA currently plays a significant role in delaying federal actions. This lack of data is attributable to the fact that, other than the Department of Energy and DOT, federal agencies do not routinely maintain information on the time it takes to complete the NEPA process. Therefore, gathering accurate data on how long it takes to prepare NEPA documentation, and whether the NEPA process is directly the cause of project delays, is difficult. For example, the preparation of NEPA documentation is generally done concurrently with preliminary project design. If a project undergoes specification changes, those alterations may necessitate modifications to the NEPA documentation. Consequently, the time to complete the NEPA process may be extended.

The perception that NEPA results in extensive delays and additional costs to the successful delivery of certain federal projects can be magnified when compliance with multiple environmental laws and regulations is required (see "The Use of NEPA as an "Umbrella" Statute," above). The sometimes extensive reviews, documentation, and analysis required by agencies such as the Army Corps of Engineers, the U.S. Fish and Wildlife Service, the Coast Guard, and EPA, as well as various state regulatory and review agencies, add further to the perception that extensive delays are related to the NEPA process. Such "delays" may actually stem from an agency's need to complete a permit process or analyses required under separate statutory authority (e.g., the Clean Water Act or Endangered Species Act), over which the lead agency has no authority.

Litigation is probably the most often cited cause of NEPA-related project delays. Although this may have been the case in the past, the total number of NEPA-related cases in the past 10 years has been small (especially when compared with the total number of federal actions requiring some environmental review under NEPA). For example, in 2005, a total of 118 NEPA-related cases were filed. Of those, 43 resulted in an injunction. The majority of cases were filed against two agencies—the USDA's Forest Service (with 50 cases files) and the Department of the Interior's Bureau of Land Management (with 12 cases files).[85] The main reason that plaintiffs filed suit was because they believed that the EIS or EA was inadequate (e.g., information was incomplete or the document did not sufficiently analyze the cumulative or indirect effects of an action).

NEPA litigation began to decline in the mid 1970s and has remained relatively constant since the late 1980s.[86] This trend may be due in part to improved agency compliance with promulgated regulations and improved agency expertise in preparing required documentation. However, another factor may be the decrease in the number of federal actions funded by Congress that would be defined as "major federal actions" under NEPA.[87]

Although litigation has decreased, agency concern regarding the threat of litigation may still affect the NEPA process, particularly for complex or controversial projects. In addition to CEQ regulations and an agency's own regulations, a project sponsor may be mindful of previous judicial interpretation when preparing NEPA documentation in an attempt to prepare a "litigation-proof" EIS. CEQ has observed that such an effort may lead to an increase in the cost and time needed to complete NEPA documentation, but not necessarily an improvement in the quality of the documents ultimately produced.[88]

## Studies into NEPA's Effectiveness and Causes of Delays

In the past 20 years, numerous surveys and reports, conducted by both public agencies and private organizations, have studied the effectiveness of the NEPA process. They sought to determine issues such as how the NEPA process is implemented at individual agencies, whether the NEPA process delays project implementation, and, if so, how those delays may be addressed and NEPA more effectively implemented.

In 2004, a survey of staff from the Department of Defense, the Department of the Interior, and the Forest Service sought to determine the degree to which the NEPA process slowed decision making and delayed projects.[89] The survey identified the following primary reasons for project delays:

- Decision maker changes in the project.
- Court challenges to a project.
- Poor documentation that needed to be redone.

- Changes in or additions to project alternatives.
- Compliance requirements of the Endangered Species Act.

Depending on the agency responding, factors "outside the NEPA process" were identified as the cause of delay between 68% and 84% of the time.

In 1997, CEQ published a study to determine NEPA's effectiveness and methods to improve its implementation.[90] Study participants included individuals and organizations that were knowledgeable about NEPA and could be characterized as both supporters and critics of NEPA. Generally, participants felt that NEPA's enduring legacy was that it provided a framework for collaboration between federal agencies and those who will bear the environmental, social, and economic impacts of agency decisions. However, they also felt that NEPA often takes too long and costs too much, agencies make decisions before hearing from the public, documents are too long and technical for many people to use, and training for agency officials is inadequate at times. Participants felt that critical elements of efficient NEPA implementation included the extent to which an agency integrates NEPA's goals into its internal planning processes at an early stage and provides information to the public.

The study found that the extent to which the public is involved in the decision-making process also influences the potential for litigation. The study also found that some states, citizen groups, and businesses believe that certain EAs are prepared to avoid public involvement (i.e., because public meetings are not always required for EAs). The preparation of an EA, rather than an EIS, is reportedly the most common source of conflict and litigation under NEPA.[91] The study further found that nongovernmental organizations (NGOs) and citizens viewed the NEPA process as a one-way communication process, skeptical that their input was effectively incorporated into agency decision making and hypothesizing that their involvement was often solicited after decisions regarding actions and alternatives have already been made. Citizens also reported being frustrated when they were treated as adversaries rather than welcome participants in the NEPA process. Citizens reported that they often felt overwhelmed by the resources available to project proponents and agencies. As a consequence, litigation may be seen as the only means to affect environmental decisions significantly.[92]

In 2002, a comprehensive study of the NEPA process was conducted by CEQ's NEPA Task Force. CEQ formed the Task Force to review NEPA implementation practices and procedures and to determine opportunities to improve and modernize the process. The Task Force interviewed federal agencies; reviewed public comments, literature, and case studies; and spoke with individuals and representatives from state and local governments, tribes, and interest groups. In 2003, the Task Force released a report of its findings and recommendations.[93]

In compiling its research, the Task Force received more than 739 stakeholder comments. Those comments reflected current issues and challenges to NEPA implementation. With regard to delays in and the effectiveness of the NEPA process, a large percentage of comments were directed at factors related to NEPA analysis and documentation requirements and to the role and effects of litigation. According to CEQ, many respondents expressed a belief that the general requirement to provide adequate analysis had been taken to an extreme; that documents had become too time-consuming and costly to produce; and that the resultant "analysis paralysis" forestalled appropriate management of public lands and ultimately left the public distrustful and disengaged. The stakeholders felt this was brought on by vague requirements that were open to considerable interpretation and, therefore, an easy target for litigation. Because the requirements were vague, those commenters further felt that agencies were not sure how much analysis would be considered adequate by the courts, resulting in pressure to produce more.

In contrast, other respondents felt the "analysis paralysis" scenario was a misnomer. These respondents believed that agencies often predetermine the outcome of the planning process, that they often fail to consider other reasonable alternatives, and that the analysis agencies provide is often inadequate to support the management plan they propose. These commenters felt that the environmental effects of proposed actions are often inadequately considered, particularly the cumulative effects; that agencies rely on inadequate or outdated data; and that agency research is not held to the same rigorous standards as research in other fields, particularly in terms of scientific reference and peer review. Moreover, they felt that agencies are sometimes intent on following a predetermined course of action and ignore concerns submitted by the public. With regard to the role of litigation, a number of respondents felt that litigation only results when agencies do not comply with NEPA requirements. Some felt that it is only through litigation that concerned parties can get agencies to recognize their concerns and give serious attention to the environmental effects of their proposed actions.

One issue discussed in the Task Force report was challenges faced by agencies with regard to budget, training, and staffing constraints. This issue is discussed in more depth in a report, cited by the Task Force, that was prepared by the Natural Resources Council (an environmental conservation organization). That report surveyed 12 federal agencies to determine how they implemented the NEPA process.[94] Included in the report was a finding that, due to budget and staff constraints, most agencies' NEPA offices lack an ongoing national tracking system to monitor the numbers and types of NEPA documents that their agency is preparing or has completed. Also, the report found that agencies were unable to document their NEPA workload, calculate average preparation times or costs, show trends in these factors over time, or respond objectively to assertions that excessive time or money is being spent on complying with NEPA's requirements. The absence of such information, the report asserted, leaves agencies in a weak position to respond factually to or critically evaluate administrative or legislative proposals to "streamline" the NEPA process (see discussion, below).

## Efforts to Streamline the NEPA Process

Some Members of Congress have expressed concerns that project delays are the result of inefficient interagency coordination required for large, complex projects. As a result, in the 108$^{th}$ Congress, several laws were enacted that included provisions intended to streamline the NEPA process. Although not defined in any of the legislation, the term "streamlining" was broadly used to describe legislative or administrative procedures intended to expedite the NEPA process.[95] It usually refers to a process or procedures to better coordinate federal, state, tribal, or local agency action, when compliance with multiple environmental laws, regulations, or executive orders is required.

In 2008, most agencies filed fewer than 10 EISs.[96] Just over 63% of all EISs were filed by seven agencies—USDA-Forest Service (124); DOT's Federal Highway Administration (64) and Federal Transit Administration (21); the Department of the Interior's Bureau of Land Management (48) and National Park Service (25); the Department of Defense's Army Corps of Engineers (42), and the Department of Energy's Federal Energy Regulatory Commission (19). It may not be surprising, then, that many streamlining activities involve actions sponsored by those agencies. For example, what follows are bills enacted since the 108$^{th}$ Congress[97] and selected types of projects for which streamlining provisions have been included:

- The Healthy Forests Restoration Act of 2003 (P.L. 108-148): "hazardous fuel reduction" projects on federal land.

- Vision 100-Century of Aviation Reauthorization Act (P.L. 108-176): airport capacity enhancement projects at congested airports.
- The Safe, Accountable, Flexible, and Efficient Transportation Equity Act of 2005: A Legacy for Users (P.L. 108-59): construction of or modifications to surface transportation projects.
- The Energy Policy Act of 2005 (P.L. 108-58): various energy development projects, such as oil and gas leasing and permitting on federal land, and the designation of energy facility rights-of-way and corridors on federal lands.
- The Water Resources Development Act (WRDA) of 2007 (P.L. 110-114): water resources projects undertaken by the Army Corps of Engineers.

Streamlining provisions are unique to the class of projects at issue. However, most include some or all of the following elements:

- The designation of specific projects as categorical exclusions.
- The designation of a specific agency as the "lead agency" for all classes of certain actions (e.g., delegation of DOT as the lead agency for all highway or transit projects requiring review under NEPA).
- Direction to the lead agency to develop a "coordinated environmental review" process to ensure early coordination and cooperation among federal, state, tribal, and local agencies required to participate in a project.
- Delegation of specific authority to the lead agency, such as the authority to establish deadlines for cooperating agencies, specify a project's "purpose and need," or specify project alternatives.
- Delegation of certain federal authority to state or local agencies (e.g., the authority to determine whether certain classes of projects may be categorically excluded from environmental requirements).
- Direction to the lead agency to develop dispute resolution procedures if agencies reach an impasse in the NEPA process.

Streamlining proposals have generated a great deal of controversy among interested stakeholders (e.g., agency representatives, industry groups, and environmental organizations). Most stakeholders agree that the process for complying with environmental requirements applicable to complex federal projects can be implemented more efficiently. How that should be done and the degree to which it is necessary have been the subject of considerable debate. Some stakeholders, such as industry representatives who would like to see projects implemented more quickly, argue that the authority of lead agencies must be strengthened to reduce delays caused by disagreements among agencies. They also contend that lead agencies should have the authority to set and enforce deadlines with regard to the cooperating agency decision-making process. Environmental groups are concerned that by speeding up the compliance process and strengthening lead agency authority, concerns of the public or cooperating agencies will be minimized or ignored, in effect rubber stamping lead agency decisions. Further, some environmental groups contend that "streamlining" is a thinly veiled attempt at weakening environmental protection and reducing public participation in the federal decision-making process.

## CONCLUSION

NEPA is a procedural statute that, along with CEQ and individual agencies' regulations, specifies procedures that must be followed in the federal decision-making process. It imposes no requirement other than to require agencies to consider the environmental impacts of their actions before proceeding with them and to involve the public in that process. It does not dictate what the decision must be. More specifically, it does not require the agency to select the least environmentally harmful alternative or to elevate environmental concerns above others.

The role the courts have played in NEPA's implementation is arguably more pronounced compared to many other environmental laws because of several unique factors. These include the initial lack of binding regulations applicable to the EIS preparation process, the absence of an agency authorized to enforce its requirements, and NEPA's requirement to involve the public in the decision-making process. With regard to the latter, when members of the public oppose a project or feel that their opinions are not given sufficient weight, their involvement may result in turning to the courts to halt the project until their concerns are addressed. During the past 35 years, interested stakeholders have challenged the adequacy of NEPA documentation and agency compliance with NEPA in court and, in some instances, used NEPA litigation to try to halt or slow projects to which they were opposed. As a result, the progress of some federal projects was slowed. However, particularly in the past 10-15 years, the number of projects affected by NEPArelated litigation is very small. Also, unlike other environmental laws, NEPA itself cannot stop a project altogether. This does not mean that, during the course of a NEPA-related lawsuit, an agency may not decide to abandon a given project or project alternative.

As a policy statute, NEPA supplements other statutes. Consequently, agencies often are required to comply with provisions of other state, tribal, and federal environmental requirements before they can proceed with a given action. This requirement can lead to confusion when procedures to comply with other laws are integrated with NEPA compliance, and it can give the impression that NEPA alone is responsible for the time it takes to obtain the appropriate authorization or approval for a federal project.

Although stakeholders disagree about the extent to which NEPA currently halts or delays federal actions, few disagree that agencies can improve their methods of NEPA compliance. Many elements of recent legislative proposals intended to streamline NEPA compliance already exist in CEQ's regulations. Those include integrating NEPA early in the planning process, integrating NEPA requirements with other environmental requirements, eliminating duplication with state and local procedures, swiftly addressing disputes with other agencies, and establishing appropriate time limits on the EIS process. Debate is likely to continue with regard to if or to what degree further streamlining may be accomplished.

## SELECTED REFERENCES

Bear, Dinah. "NEPA at 19: A Primer on an 'Old' Law with Solutions to New Problems," 19 *Environmental Law Reporter* 10060, February 1989.

Caldwell, Lynton. *The National Environmental Policy Act: An Agenda for the Future*. Bloomington, IN: Indiana University Press, 1998.

Council on Environmental Quality. "Forty Most Asked Questions Concerning CEQ's National Environmental Policy Act Regulations," 46 *Federal Register* 18026, March 23, 1981.

Council on Environmental Quality. "Memorandum for General Counsels, NEPA Liaisons and Participants in Scoping," April 20, 1981.

Council on Environmental Quality. "The National Environmental Policy Act: A Study of Its Effectiveness After Twenty-five Years," January 1997.

Council on Environmental Quality's NEPA Task Force. "Report to the Council on Environmental Quality: Modernizing NEPA Implementation," September 2003.

Smythe, Robert and Isber, Caroline. "NEPA in the Agencies: 2002, A Report to the Natural Resources Council of America," October 2002.

## End Notes

[1] CEQ is charged with providing oversight and guidance to agencies with regard to EIS preparation. The Environmental Protection Agency (EPA) is required to review and comment publicly on the environmental impacts of proposed federal activities, including those for which an EIS is prepared. EPA is also the official recipient of all EISs prepared by federal agencies. However, neither agency has enforcement authority with regard to an agency's environmental review requirements.

[2] S.Rept. 91-296, 91st Cong., 1st sess., July 9, 1969, pp. 11-12, and Lynton Caldwell, *The National Environmental Policy Act: An Agenda for the Future*, Indiana University Press, 1998, pp. 26-27.

[3] Statement by Governor Rockefeller in *Joint House-Senate Colloquium to Discuss a National Policy for the Environment, Hearing before the Committee on Interior and Insular Affairs, United States Senate, and the Committee on Science and Astronautics, U.S. House of Representatives*, July 17, 1968, p. 5.

[4] "Congressional White Paper on a National Policy for the Environment," issued jointly by the Committee on Interior and Insular Affairs, United States Senate, and the Committee on Science and Astronautics, U.S. House of Representatives, summarizing key points raised in the dialog, October 1968, Committee Print, p. 9.

[5] S. 1075 was introduced by Senator Jackson on February 18, 1969. H.R. 12549 was introduced by Representative John Dingell, and others, on July 1, 1969.

[6] Senator Jackson's remarks regarding "S. 1075—Introduction of Bill to Establish a National Strategy for the Management of the Human Environment," vol. 115, *Congressional Record*, p. S1780, February 18, 1969 (reprinted in *National Environmental Policy Act of 1969: Legislative History, Senate bill 1075, Public law 91-190, 91st Congress, 1st session*, James D. Nuse, compiler, for the U.S. Atomic Energy Commission, September 1970).

[7] Although several similar bills were introduced in the Senate that session, those that ultimately received consideration by the Committee were S. 1075, S. 237 (which included a declaration of environmental policy) and S. 1752.

[8] Dr. Caldwell is a Professor of Public and Environmental Affairs at Indiana University and was a staff consultant to the Senate Committee on Interior and Insular Affairs on a National Policy for the Environment, 1968-1970.

[9] *Hearing before the Committee on Interior and Insular Affairs, United States Senate, 91st Congress, 1st Session, on S. 1075, S. 237, and S. 1752*, April 16, 1969, p. 116.

[10] Ibid., p. 117.

[11] S. 1075 Amendments, referred to Senate Committee on Interior and Insular Affairs, May 29, 1969.

[12] Section 102(C), S. 1075 Amendments, May 29, 1969.

[13] S.Rept. 91-296, p. 14.

[14] NEPA was amended by P.L. 94-52, July 3, 1975, regarding how CEQ may spend appropriated funds; P.L. 94-83, August 9, 1975, specifying parameters under which states may prepare an EIS; and P.L. 97-258, § 4(b), September 13, 1982, regarding budget and accounting procedures.

[15] 42 U.S.C. § 7609.
[16] 42 U.S.C. § 4331.
[17] 42 U.S.C. § 4331(b).
[18] 42 U.S.C. § 4332(2)(C).
[19] Ibid.
[20] 42 U.S.C. § 4332(2)(E).
[21] 42 U.S.C. § 4333.
[22] 42 U.S.C. § 4335.
[23] 42 U.S.C. § 4341. The 1997 Environmental Quality Report was the last one prepared by CEQ. The Federal Reports Elimination and Sunset Act of 1995 (P.L. 104-66) eliminated many congressionally mandated reports, including the annual CEQ Environmental Quality Report, unless explicitly requested by Congress.
[24] Lynton Caldwell, *The National Environmental Policy Act: An Agenda for the Future*, Indiana University Press, 1998, p. 2.
[25] For an analysis of legal issues, consult the American Law Division of CRS.
[26] *Baltimore Gas & Electric Co. v. Natural Resources Defense Council, Inc.*, 462 U.S. 87, 97, 100 (1983).
[27] *Robertson v. Methow Valley Citizens Council*, 490 U.S. 332 (1989).
[28] Ibid., at 351.
[29] Executive Order 11514, Protection and Enhancement of Environmental Quality, signed by President Nixon, March 5, 1970, 35 *Federal Register* 4247.
[30] H.Rept. 92-316, "Administration of the National Environmental Policy Act," June 1971.
[31] Dinah Bear (CEQ General Counsel), "NEPA at 19: A Primer on an 'Old' Law with Solutions to New Problems," 19 *Environmental Law Reporter* 10060, p. 10062, February 1989.
[32] Dinah Bear, "The National Environmental Policy Act: Its Origins and Evolutions," *Natural Resources & Environment*, vol. 10, no. 2, fall 1995, p. 70.
[33] Executive Order 11991, Relating to Protection and Enhancement of Environmental Quality, signed by President Carter, May 24, 1977, 42 *Federal Register* 26967.
[34] 43 *Federal Register* 55978, November 28, 1978; 40 C.F.R. §§ 1500-1508.
[35] Council on Environmental Quality, *Ninth Annual Report of the Council on Environmental Quality*, December 1978, pp. 396-399; and at 40 C.F.R. §§ 1500.4 and 1500.5.
[36] 40 C.F.R. § 1500.1.
[37] 40 C.F.R. § 1507.3.
[38] 40 C.F.R. § 1500.6.
[39] The "Forty Most Asked Questions" and other CEQ guidance are available at http://ceq.hss.doe.gov/nepa/regs/ guidance.html
[40] The guidance is available at http://www.whitehouse.gov/administration/eop/ceq/ initiatives/nepa.
[41] The CEQ regulations, at 40 C.F.R. § 1508.18, specify that the term "major" in the phrase "major federal action" reinforces but does not have meaning independent of "significantly." This discussion focuses on criteria used to determine whether the level of federal agency involvement in an action is such that the action is federalized and, when it is, the categories of action subject to NEPA. Criteria used to determine if environmental impacts are significant are discussed in "Determining the Significance of a Federal Action" section, below.
[42] 40 C.F.R. § 1508.18(a).

[43] 40 C.F.R. § 1508.18(b)(4). Further, the term "federal agency" is defined as all agencies of the federal government but does not mean the Congress, the Judiciary, or the President (40 C.F.R. § 1508.12).

[44] Sixteen states, the District of Columbia, Puerto Rico, and some municipalities and tribal governments have enacted their own environmental quality acts, sometimes referred to as "little NEPAs." For a list of the 16 states and corresponding citations to relevant state law, see the State Environmental Resource Center (SERC) web page regarding State Environmental Quality Acts at http://www.serconline.org/SEQA/stateactivity.html.

[45] Determining the level of federal involvement that would federalize a private project is becoming more relevant as state and local governments are increasingly turning to public-private partnerships to fill gaps in federal funding for needed projects (e.g., surface transportation projects, school maintenance, and construction projects).

[46] The tiering process is discussed at 40 C.F.R. § 1502.20; also, see answers to questions 24a-c regarding EISs required on policies, plans, or programs in CEQ's "Forty Most Asked Questions."

[47] 40 C.F.R. § 1508.17.

[48] 40 C.F.R. § 1508.27.

[49] 40 C.F.R. § 1508.27(a).

[50] 40 C.F.R. § 1508.27(b).

[51] CEQ's "Number of EIS filed with EPA by Federal Agencies," available at http://ceq.hss.doe.gov/nepa/nepanet.htm.

[52] See "FHWA Projects by Class of Action," on FHWA's "Streamlining/Stewardship" Website, available at http://environment.fhwa.dot.gov/strmlng/projectgraphs.asp.

[53] 40 C.F.R. § 1508.22.

[54] 40 C.F.R. § 1501.7.

[55] 40 C.F.R. § 1502.9.

[56] 40 C.F.R. § 1502.14.

[57] See answer to question 2a regarding Alternatives Outside the Capability of Applicant or Jurisdiction of Agency in CEQ's guidance document "Forty Most Asked Questions."

[58] Ibid., answer to question 1b regarding how many alternatives have to be discussed when there is an infinite number of possible alternatives.

[59] 40 C.F.R. § 1505.2.

[60] Copies of this documentation are generally available from the lead agency. Often, particularly for EISs, NEPA documentation is available on an agency's website.

[61] 40 C.F.R. § 1508.9(a).

[62] 40 C.F.R. § 1508.9(b).

[63] 40 C.F.R. § 1501.4(e)(1).

[64] 40 C.F.R. § 1507.3.

[65] 23 C.F.R. § 771.117.

[66] 40 C.F.R. § 1508.4.

[67] The guidance is available online at http://www.whitehouse.gov/administration/eop/ceq/initiatives/nepa.

[68] 40 C.F.R. § 1508.16.

[69] A project applicant may be any public or private entity initiating a "federal" action. For example, a state department of transportation may initiate the NEPA process for a federally funded surface transportation project. A project applicant may also be a private entity requesting a federal permit. For example, a livestock owner applying for a permit to graze cattle on federal land may also initiate the NEPA process. The lead agency in such a case

would be the federal agency (e.g., the U.S. Department of Agriculture's Forest Service) issuing the permit.

[70] 40 C.F.R. § 1508.5.

[71] Text of Secretary Mineta's May 6, 2003 letter, and Chairman Connaughton's May 12, 2003 response, are available at http://www.environment.fhwa.dot.gov/guidebook/ Ginterim.asp.

[72] 42 U.S.C. § 4332(2)(C).

[73] 40 C.F.R. § 1503.

[74] 40 C.F.R. § 1503.1.

[75] 40 C.F.R. §1503.4.

[76] NEPA documentation is required of EPA for research and development activities, facility construction, wastewater treatment plant construction under the Clean Water Act, EPA-issued National Pollutant Discharge Elimination System (NPDES) permits, and certain projects funded through EPA annual appropriations acts. For more information about EPA's requirements with regard to NEPA compliance, see http://www.epa.gov/compliance/ nepa/epacompliance/ index.html.

[77] See an explanation of EPA's "Environmental Impact Statement (EIS) Rating System Criteria" at http://www.epa.gov/compliance/nepa/comments/ratings.html.

[78] 40 C.F.R. §1504.1.

[79] 40 C.F.R. §1504.2.

[80] Although the MOA is not readily available, reference to it and the allocation of duties between EPA and CEQ is discussed in a March 7, 1989, *Federal Register* notice available on EPA's Compliance and Enforcement website under "EIS Filing System," at http://www.epa.gov/ compliance/resources/policies/nepa/index.html.

[81] 40 C.F.R. § 1500.2(d).

[82] 40 C.F.R. § 1506.6.

[83] Council on Environmental Quality, *The National Environmental Policy Act: A Study of Its Effectiveness After Twenty-five Years*, January 1997, p. ix.

[84] 40 C.F.R. § 1502.25.

[85] See, Council on Environmental Quality "2005 Litigation Survey," available at http://ceq.eh.doe.gov/nepa/ nepanet.htm.

[86] See Council on Environmental Quality, *Environmental Quality: 25th Anniversary Report* (the CEQ 1994-95 Annual Report) 1996, p. 51, available at http://ceq.eh.doe.gov/nepa/reports/ reports.htm, and Litigation Surveys for 2001 through 2005, available at http://ceq.eh.doe.gov/nepa/nepanet.htm.

[87] Dinah Bear, "NEPA at 19," 19 *ELR* 10062.

[88] Council on Environmental Quality, "NEPA Study of Effectiveness After Twenty-five Years," p. iii.

[89] The survey, *Fast Tracking NEPA Documents—Tools to Overcome Schedule Delays,* was conducted in 2003 and 2004 by Tetra Tech, Inc., for presentation at the 30th National Defense Industrial Association Environmental and Energy Symposium and Exhibition. The survey includes responses from agency staff identified as NEPA project managers, NEPA resource authors, agency NEPA officers or reviews, or non-NEPA professionals, such as engineers. Results are available at http://www.dtic.mil/ndia/2004enviro/, under April 7, 2004, Session Nine.

[90] Council on Environmental Quality, "NEPA Study of Effectiveness After Twenty-five Years."

[91] Ibid., p. 19.

[92] Ibid., p. 18.

[93] "The NEPA Task Force Report to the Council on Environmental Quality: Modernizing NEPA Implementation," September 2003, and comments documented by the Task Force are available at http://ceq.eh.doe.gov/ntf/index.html.

[94] Robert Smythe and Caroline Isber, "NEPA in the Agencies: 2002, A Report to the Natural Resources Council of America," October 2002, available at http://www.naturalresources council.org/ewebeditpro/items/O89F2656.pdf. Many of the findings regarding agency implementation of NEPA and recommendations for change were directed to the CEQ NEPA Task Force.

[95] The term "streamlining" has also been used to refer to administrative or legislative actions intended to expedite the process of complying with other environmental requirements, such as permitting.

[96] See the Council on Environmental Quality's "Number of EIS filed with EPA by Federal Agencies" for 2008, available at http://ceq.hss.doe.gov/nepa/ Calendar_Year_2008_ Filed_EISs.pdf.

[97] Since 2007, there have been various legislative proposals with provisions intended to expedite the NEPA process or waive NEPA requirements for certain classes of federal action, but few legislative proposals have progressed beyond their introduction.

In: The National Environmental Policy Act
Editor: Sabrina Reynolds
ISBN: 978-1-63321-464-4


*Chapter 2*

# NATIONAL ENVIRONMENTAL POLICY ACT: LITTLE INFORMATION EXISTS ON NEPA ANALYSES*

*United States Government Accountability Office*

## WHY GAO DID THIS STUDY

NEPA requires all federal agencies to evaluate the potential environmental effects of proposed projects—such as roads or bridges—on the human environment. Agencies prepare an EIS when a project will have a potentially significant impact on the environment. They may prepare an EA to determine whether a project will have a significant potential impact. If a project fits within a category of activities determined to have no significant impact—a CE— then an EA or an EIS is generally not necessary. The adequacy of these analyses has been a focus of litigation.

GAO was asked to review various issues associated with completing NEPA analyses. This report describes information on the (1) number and type of NEPA analyses, (2) costs and benefits of completing those analyses, and (3) frequency and outcomes of related litigation. GAO included available information on both costs and benefits to be consistent with standard economic principles for evaluating federal programs, and selected the Departments of

* This is an edited, reformatted and augmented version of the United States Government Accountability Office publication, GAO-14-370, dated April 2014.

Defense, Energy, the Interior, and Transportation, and the USDA Forest Service for analysis because they generally complete the most NEPA analyses. GAO reviewed documents and interviewed individuals from federal agencies, academia, and professional groups with expertise in NEPA analyses and litigation. GAO's findings are not generalizeable to agencies other than those selected.

This report has no recommendations. GAO provided a draft to CEQ and agency officials for review and comment, and they generally agreed with GAO's findings.

## What GAO Found

Governmentwide data on the number and type of most National Environmental Policy Act (NEPA) analyses are not readily available, as data collection efforts vary by agency. NEPA generally requires federal agencies to evaluate the potential environmental effects of actions they propose to carry out, fund, or approve (e.g., by permit) by preparing analyses of different comprehensiveness depending on the significance of a proposed project's effects on the environment—from the most detailed Environmental Impact Statements (EIS) to the less comprehensive Environmental Assessments (EA) and Categorical Exclusions (CE). Agencies do not routinely track the number of EAs or CEs, but the Council on Environmental Quality (CEQ)—the entity within the Executive Office of the President that oversees NEPA implementation—estimates that about 95 percent of NEPA analyses are CEs, less than 5 percent are EAs, and less than 1 percent are EISs. Projects requiring an EIS are a small portion of all projects but are likely to be high-profile, complex, and expensive. The Environmental Protection Agency (EPA) maintains governmentwide information on EISs. A 2011 Congressional Research Service report noted that determining the total number of federal actions subject to NEPA is difficult, since most agencies track only the number of actions requiring an EIS.

Little information exists on the costs and benefits of completing NEPA analyses. Agencies do not routinely track the cost of completing NEPA analyses, and there is no governmentwide mechanism to do so, according to officials from CEQ, EPA, and other agencies GAO reviewed. However, the Department of Energy (DOE) tracks limited cost data associated with NEPA analyses. DOE officials told GAO that they track the money the agency pays to contractors to conduct NEPA analyses. According to DOE data, its median

EIS contractor cost for calendar years 2003 through 2012 was $1.4 million. For context, a 2003 task force report to CEQ—the only available source of governmentwide cost estimates— estimated that a typical EIS cost from $250,000 to $2 million. EAs and CEs generally cost less than EISs, according to CEQ and federal agencies. Information on the benefits of completing NEPA analyses is largely qualitative. According to studies and agency officials, some of the qualitative benefits of NEPA include its role in encouraging public participation and in discovering and addressing project design problems that could be more costly in the long run. Complicating the determination of costs and benefits, agency activities under NEPA are hard to separate from other required environmental analyses under federal laws such as the Endangered Species Act and the Clean Water Act; executive orders; agency guidance; and state and local laws.

Some information is available on the frequency and outcome of NEPA litigation. Agency data, interviews with agency officials, and available studies show that most NEPA analyses do not result in litigation, although the impact of litigation could be substantial if a single lawsuit affects numerous federal decisions or actions in several states. In 2011, the most recent data available, CEQ reported 94 NEPA cases filed, down from the average of 129 cases filed per year from calendar year 2001 through calendar year 2008. The federal government prevails in most NEPA litigation, according to CEQ and legal studies.

## ABBREVIATIONS

| | |
|---|---|
| BLM | Bureau of Land Management |
| CE | Categorical Exclusion |
| CEQ | Council on Environmental Quality |
| CRS | Congressional Research Service |
| DOD | Department of Defense |
| DOE | Department of Energy |
| DOT | Department of Transportation |
| eMNEPA | electronic Management of NEPA |
| EA | Environmental Assessment |
| EIS | Environmental Impact Statement |
| EPA | Environmental Protection Agency |
| FHWA | Federal Highway Administration |
| NAEP | National Association of Environmental Professionals |

| | |
|---|---|
| NEPA | National Environmental Policy Act |
| PAPAI | Project and Program Action Information |
| PEPC | Planning, Environment, and Public Comment |

April 15, 2014

The Honorable Peter DeFazio
Ranking Member
Committee on Natural Resources
House of Representatives

The Honorable Edward Markey
United States Senate

The National Environmental Policy Act (NEPA)—the statute requiring federal agencies to evaluate the potential environmental effects of proposed projects on the human environment—has been identified by critics as a cause of delay for projects because of time-consuming requirements and praised by proponents for, among other things, bringing public participation into government decision making.[1] Under NEPA, all federal agencies generally are to evaluate the potential environmental effects of actions they propose to carry out, fund, or approve (e.g., by permit)—including the development of infrastructure projects, such as roads and bridges. Enacted in 1970, NEPA, and the subsequent Council on Environmental Quality Regulations Implementing the Procedural Provisions of NEPA, set out an environmental review process that has two principal purposes: (1) to ensure that an agency carefully considers information concerning the potential environmental effects of proposed development projects and (2) to ensure that this information is made available to the public.[2] NEPA requires federal agencies to analyze the nature and extent of a project's potential environmental effects and, in many cases, document these analyses.[3] The documentation and comprehensiveness of these analyses depends on the significance of a project's potential effects on the environment. The adequacy of NEPA analyses has been a focus of litigation. You asked us to review various issues associated with completing NEPA analyses. This report describes information on the (1) number and type of NEPA analyses, (2) costs and benefits of completing those analyses, and (3) frequency and outcomes of related litigation. We included available information on both costs and benefits to be consistent with standard economic principles for evaluating federal programs and generally accepted government auditing standards.

To respond to these objectives, we reviewed relevant publications, obtained documents and analyses from federal agencies, and interviewed federal officials and individuals from academia and professional associations with expertise in conducting NEPA analyses. Specifically, to describe the number and type of NEPA analyses from calendar year 2008 through calendar year 2012 and what is known about the costs and benefits of NEPA analyses, we reported information identified through the literature review, interviews, and other sources. We selected the Departments of Defense, Energy, the Interior, and Transportation; and the Forest Service within the U.S. Department of Agriculture for analysis because they generally complete the most NEPA analyses. Our findings for these agencies are not generalizeable to other federal agencies but provide examples of NEPA implementation. To describe the frequency and outcome of NEPA litigation, we reviewed (1) laws, regulations, and agency guidance; (2) NEPA litigation data collected from federal entities and the National Association of Environmental Professionals (NAEP), the professional association for NEPA practitioners within and outside the federal government; and (3) relevant studies. To assess the reliability of data collected from the selected agencies, we reviewed existing documentation when available and interviewed officials, including those from the U.S. Department of Justice, knowledgeable about the data. We found all data to be sufficiently reliable for the purposes of this report. See appendix I for additional details on our objectives, scope, and methodology.

We conducted this performance audit from June 2013 to April 2014 in accordance with generally accepted government auditing standards. Those standards require that we plan and perform the audit to obtain sufficient, appropriate evidence to provide a reasonable basis for our findings and conclusions based on our audit objectives. We believe that the evidence obtained provides a reasonable basis for our findings and conclusions based on our audit objectives.

## Background

Under NEPA, federal agencies generally are to evaluate the likely environmental effects of projects they are proposing by preparing either an Environmental Assessment (EA) or a more detailed Environmental Impact Statement (EIS), assuming no Categorical Exclusion (CE) applies. Agencies may prepare an EA to determine whether a proposed project is expected to have a potentially significant impact on the human environment.[4] If prior to or during the development of an EA, the agency determines that the project may cause significant environmental impacts, an EIS should be prepared. However, if the agency, in its EA, determines there are no significant impacts from the proposed project or action, then it is to prepare a document—a Finding of No Significant Impact—that presents the reasons why the agency has concluded that no significant environmental impacts will occur if the project is implemented. An EIS is a more detailed statement than an EA, and NEPA implementing regulations specify requirements and procedures—such as providing the public with an opportunity to comment on the draft document—applicable to the EIS process that are not mandated for EAs.[5]

If a proposed project fits within a category of activities that an agency has already determined normally does not have the potential for significant environmental impacts—a CE—and the agency has established that category of activities in its NEPA implementing procedures, then it generally need not prepare an EA or EIS.[6] The agency may instead approve projects that fit within the relevant category by using one of its established CEs. For example, the Bureau of Land Management (BLM) within the Department of the Interior (Interior) has CEs in place for numerous types of activities, such as constructing nesting platforms for wild birds and constructing snow fences for safety. For a project to be approved using a CE, the agency must determine whether any extraordinary circumstances exist in which a normally excluded action may have a significant effect. Figure 1 illustrates the general process for implementing NEPA requirements.

Private individuals or companies may become involved in the NEPA process when a project they are developing needs a permit or other authorization from a federal agency to proceed, such as when the project involves federal land. For example, a company may apply for such a permit in constructing a pipeline crossing federal lands; in that case, the agency that is being asked to issue the permit must evaluate the potential environmental effects of constructing the pipeline under NEPA. The private company or developer may in some cases provide environmental analyses and documentation or enter into an agreement with an agency to pay a contractor for the preparation of environmental analyses and documents, but the agency remains ultimately responsible for the scope and content of the analyses under NEPA.[7]

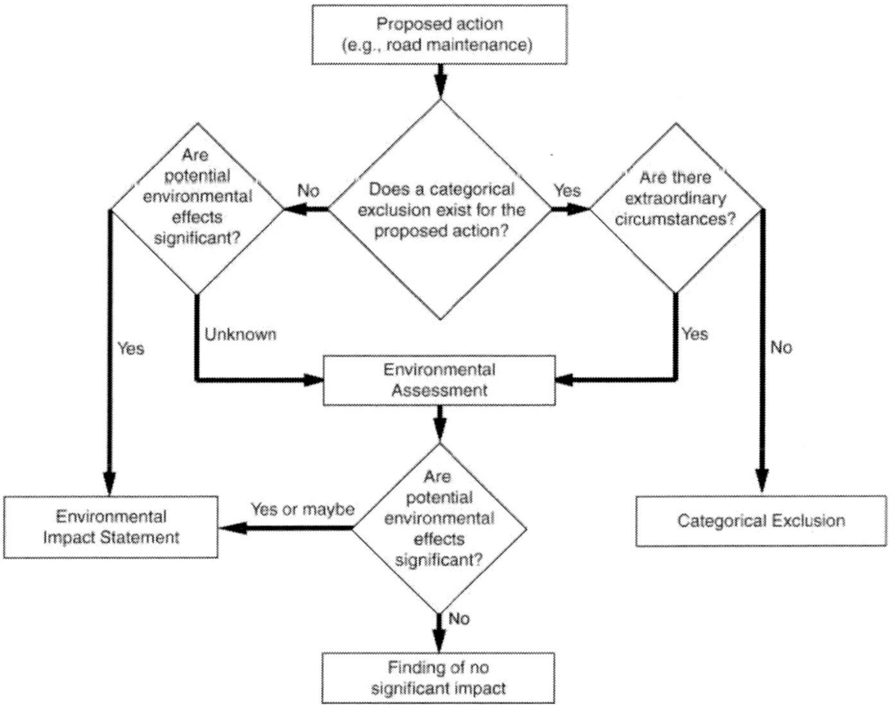


Source: GAO.

Figure 1. Process for Implementing National Environmental Policy Act Requirements.

The Council on Environmental Quality (CEQ) within the Executive Office of the President oversees the implementation of NEPA, reviews and approves federal agency NEPA procedures, and issues regulations and guidance documents that govern and guide federal agencies' interpretation and implementation of NEPA.[8] The Environmental Protection Agency (EPA) also plays two key roles in other agencies' NEPA processes. First, EPA reviews and publicly comments on the adequacy of each draft EIS and the environmental impacts of the proposed actions reviewed in the EIS. If EPA determines that the action is environmentally unsatisfactory, it is required by law to refer the matter to CEQ. Second, EPA maintains a national EIS filing system. Federal entities must publish in the Federal Register a Notice of Intent to prepare an EIS and file their draft and final EISs with EPA, which publishes weekly notices in the Federal Register listing EISs available for public review and comment.[9]

CEQ's regulations implementing NEPA require federal agencies to solicit public comment on draft EISs.[10] When the public comment period is finished, the agency proposing to carry out or permitting a project is to analyze comments, conduct further analysis as necessary, and prepare the final EIS. In the final EIS, the agency is to respond to the substantive comments received from other government agencies and the public. Sometimes a federal agency must prepare a supplemental analysis to either a draft or final EIS if it makes substantial changes in the proposed action that are relevant to environmental concerns, or if there are significant new circumstances or information relevant to environmental concerns.[11] Further, in certain circumstances, agencies may—through "incorporation by reference," "adoption," or "tiering"—use another analysis to meet some or, in the case of adoption, all of the environmental review requirements of NEPA.[12]

Unlike other environmental statutes, such as the Clean Water Act or the Clean Air Act, no individual agency has enforcement authority with regard to NEPA's implementation.[13] This absence of enforcement authority is sometimes cited as the reason that litigation has been chosen as an avenue by individuals and groups that disagree with how an agency meets NEPA requirements for a given project.[14] For example, a group may allege that an EIS is inadequate, or that the environmental impacts of an action will in fact be significant when an agency has determined they are not. Critics of NEPA have stated that those who disapprove of a federal project will use NEPA as the basis for litigation to delay or halt that project. Others argue that litigation only results when agencies do not comply with NEPA's procedural requirements.

## Data on the Number and Type of Most NEPA Analyses Are Not Readily Available

Governmentwide data on the number and type of most NEPA analyses are not readily available, as data collection efforts vary by agency (see app. II for a summary of federal NEPA data collection efforts). Agencies do not routinely track the number of EAs or CEs, but CEQ estimates that EAs and CEs comprise most NEPA analyses. EPA publishes and maintains governmentwide information on EISs.

## Many Agencies Do Not Routinely Track the Number of EAs or CEs, but CEQ Estimates That EAs and CEs Comprise Most NEPA Analyses

Many agencies do not routinely track the number of EAs or CEs. However, based on information provided to CEQ by federal agencies, CEQ estimates that about 95 percent of NEPA analyses are CEs, less than 5 percent are EAs, and less than 1 percent are EISs. These estimates were consistent with the information collected on projects funded by the American Recovery and Reinvestment Act of 2009 (Recovery Act).[15] Projects requiring an EIS are a small portion of all projects but are likely to be high-profile, complex, and expensive. As the Congressional Research Service (CRS) noted in its 2011 report on NEPA, determining the total number of federal actions subject to NEPA is difficult, since most agencies track only the number of actions requiring an EIS.[16]

The percentages of EISs, EAs, and CEs vary by agency because of differences in project type and agency mission. For example, the Department of Energy (DOE) reported that 95 percent of its 9,060 NEPA analyses from fiscal year 2008 to fiscal year 2012 were CEs, 2.6 percent were EAs, and 2.4 percent were EISs or supplement analyses. Further, in June 2012, we reported that the vast majority of highway projects are processed as CEs, noting that the Federal Highway Administration (FHWA) within the Department of Transportation (DOT) estimated that approximately 96 percent of highway projects were processed as CEs, based on data collected in 2009.[17] Representing the lowest proportion of CEs in the data available to us, the Forest Service reported that 78 percent of its 14,574 NEPA analyses from fiscal year 2008 to fiscal year 2012 were CEs, 20 percent were EAs, and 2 percent were EISs.

Of the agencies we reviewed, DOE and the Forest Service officials told us that CEs are likely underrepresented in their totals because agency systems do not track certain categories of CEs considered "routine" activities, such as emergency preparedness planning. For example, DOE officials stated that the department has two types of CEs, those that (1) are routine (e.g., administrative, financial, and personnel actions; information gathering, analysis, and dissemination) and are not tracked and (2) are documented as required by DOE regulations.

## Governmentwide Data Are Available on EISs

EPA publishes and maintains governmentwide information on EISs, updated when Notices of Availability for draft and final EISs are published in the Federal Register. CEQ and NAEP publish publicly available reports on EISs using EPA data.[18] As shown in table 1, the three compilations of EIS data produce different totals.

**Table 1. Number of Environmental Impact Statements from EPA, CEQ, and NAEP, 2008 through 2012**

| | Environmental Protection Agency (EPA) | | | Council on Environmental Quality (CEQ) | | | National Association of Environmental Professionals (NAEP) | | |
|---|---|---|---|---|---|---|---|---|---|
| **Calendar year** | **Draft** | **Final** | **Total** | **Draft** | **Final** | **Total** | **Draft** | **Final** | **Total** |
| 2008 | 270 | 277 | **547** | 270 | 277 | **547**[a] | 272 | 276 | **548**[b] |
| 2009 | 252 | 203 | **455** | 252 | 203 | **455**[c] | 277 | 222 | **499** |
| 2010 | 242 | 240 | **482** | 241 | 246 | **487** | 243 | 231 | **474** |
| 2011 | 235 | 201 | **436** | 234 | 201 | **435** | 234 | 204 | **438** |
| 2012 | 200 | 197 | **397** | 199 | 198 | **397** | 194 | 210 | **404** |
| **Total** | **1,199** | **1,118** | **2,317** | **1,196** | **1,125** | **2,321** | **1,220** | **1,143** | **2,363** |

Sources: GAO analysis of EPA data, and CEQ and NAEP reports.

Notes: NEPA calls for federal agencies to circulate a draft Environmental Impact Statement (EIS) for public review and comment. When the public comment period is finished, the agency analyzes comments, conducts further analysis as necessary, and prepares the final EIS. The final EIS is circulated for review and may be made available for public review and comment.

The differences in EIS numbers are likely due to different assumptions used to count the number of EISs and minor inconsistencies in the EPA data compiled for the CEQ and NAEP reports and GAO's analysis of EPA's database. EPA officials told us that the data it provides to others may differ because EPA periodically corrects the manually entered data in their EIS database.

[a] In 2008, two different CEQ documents listed 543 and 547 total EISs, respectively. We used the 547 value in this table because it matched the sum of the draft and final EIS reported by CEQ in 2008 and also because it matched the total number we derived from the information supplied by EPA.

[b] One section of NAEP's Annual NEPA Report 2008 identified a total of 548 EISs for 2008, while another section of the report identified a total of 547. We use 548 for this table to remain consistent with NAEP's summary of EIS data for 2008.

[c] For 2009, the CEQ source document shows 450 for the total number of EISs, but this is a computation error because the total from adding the "draft" and "final" entries is 455.

According to CEQ and EPA officials, the differences in EIS numbers shown in table 1 are likely due to different assumptions used to count the number of EISs and minor inconsistencies in the EPA data compiled for the CEQ and NAEP reports and for our analysis of EPA's data. CEQ obtains the EIS data it reports based on summary totals provided by EPA. Occasionally, CEQ also gathers some CE, EA, and EIS data through its "data call" process, by which it aggregates information submitted by agencies that use different data collection mechanisms of varying quality. According to a January 2011 CRS report on NEPA, agencies track the total draft, final, and supplemental EISs filed, not the total number of individual federal actions requiring an EIS.[19] In other words, agency data generally reflect the number of EIS documents associated with a project, not the number of projects.

Four agencies—the Forest Service, BLM, FHWA, and the U.S. Army Corps of Engineers within the Department of Defense (DOD)—are generally the most frequent producers of EISs, accounting for 60 percent of the EISs in 2012, according to data in NAEP's April 2013 report.[20] As shown in table 2, these agencies account for over half of total draft and final EISs from 2008 through 2012, according to NAEP data.

## LITTLE INFORMATION EXISTS ON THE COSTS AND BENEFITS OF COMPLETING NEPA ANALYSES

Little information exists at the agencies we reviewed on the costs and benefits of completing NEPA analyses. We found that, with few exceptions, the agencies did not routinely track data on the cost of completing NEPA analyses, and that the cost associated with conducting an EIS or EA can vary considerably, depending on the complexity and scope of the project. Information on the benefits of completing NEPA analyses is largely qualitative. Complicating matters, agency activities under NEPA are hard to separate from other environmental review tasks under federal laws, such as the Clean Water Act and the Endangered Species Act; executive orders; agency guidance; and state and local laws.

**Table 2. Number of Environmental Impact Statements by Agency as Reported by National Association of Environmental Professionals (NAEP), 2008 through 2012**

| Calendar year | Forest Service | | Bureau of Land Management[a] | | Federal Highway Administration | | Army Corps of Engineers | | All other agencies[b] | | Total |
|---|---|---|---|---|---|---|---|---|---|---|---|
| | Number | Percentage of total | Number | Percentage of total | Number | Percentage of total | Number | Percentage of total | Number | Percentage of total | |
| 2008 | 123 | 22 | 49 | 9 | 65 | 12 | 43 | 8 | 268 | 49 | **548[c]** |
| 2009 | 134 | 27 | 28 | 6 | 58 | 12 | 41 | 8 | 238 | 48 | **499** |
| 2010 | 104 | 22 | 55 | 12 | 56 | 12 | 39 | 8 | 220 | 46 | **474** |
| 2011 | 109 | 25 | 42 | 10 | 49 | 11 | 33 | 8 | 205 | 47 | **438** |
| 2012 | 102 | 25 | 56 | 14 | 44 | 11 | 41 | 10 | 161 | 40 | **404** |
| **Total** | **572** | **24** | **230** | **10** | **272** | **12** | **197** | **8** | **1,092** | **46** | **2,363** |

Source: GAO analysis of NAEP data.

Note: The National Environmental Policy Act (NEPA) calls for federal agencies to solicit input by submitting a draft Environmental Impact Statement (EIS) for public comment. When the public comment period is finished, the agency analyzes comments, conducts further analysis as necessary, and prepares the final EIS.

[a] According to BLM officials, BLM completed 53 NEPA analyses in 2010, 44 in 2011, and 20 in 2012. We present NAEP's analysis of EPA data in this table.

[b] In 2012, 31 other agencies completed at least 1 draft or final EIS. Five of them prepared 10 or more, including the National Park Service (21 draft and final EISs) and the Fish and Wildlife Service (19), both within the Department of the Interior; the National Oceanic and Atmospheric Administration within the Department of Commerce (17); the Navy within the Department of Defense (14); and the Federal Transit Administration within the Department of Transportation (10). The list of agencies varied somewhat for each of the other fiscal years presented (2008 through 2011).

[c] One section of NAEP's Annual NEPA Report 2008 identified a total of 548 EISs for 2008, while another section of the report identified a total of 547. We use 548 for this table to remain consistent with NAEP's summary of EIS data for 2008.

## Little Information Exists on the Cost of Completing NEPA Analyses

Little information exists on the cost of completing NEPA analyses. With few exceptions, the agencies we reviewed do not track the cost of completing NEPA analyses, although some of the agencies tracked information on NEPA time frames, which can be an element of project cost.

### *Most Agencies We Reviewed Do Not Track the Cost of Completing NEPA Analyses*

In general, we found that the agencies we reviewed do not routinely track data on the cost of completing NEPA analyses. According to CEQ officials, CEQ rarely collects data on projected or estimated costs related to complying with NEPA. EPA officials also told us that there is no governmentwide mechanism to track the costs of completing EISs. Similarly, most of the agencies we reviewed do not track NEPA cost data. For example, Forest Service officials said that tracking the cost of completing NEPA analyses is not currently a feature of their NEPA data collection system. Complicating efforts to record costs, applicants may, in some cases, provide environmental analyses and documentation or enter into an agreement with the agency to pay for the preparation of NEPA analyses and documentation needed for permits issued by federal agencies.[21] Agencies generally do not report costs that are "paid by the applicant" because these costs reflect business transactions between applicants and their contractors and are not available to agency officials.

Two NEPA-related studies completed by federal agencies illustrate how it is difficult to extract NEPA cost data from agency accounting systems. An August 2007 Forest Service report on competitive sourcing for NEPA compliance stated that it is "very difficult to track the actual cost of performing NEPA. Positions that perform NEPA-related activities are currently located within nearly every staff group, and are funded by a large number of budget line items. There is no single budget line item or budget object code to follow in attempting to calculate the costs of doing NEPA."[22] Similarly, a 2003 study funded by FHWA evaluating the performance of environmental "streamlining" noted that NEPA cost data would be difficult to segregate for analysis.[23]

However, DOE tracks limited cost data associated with NEPA analyses. DOE officials told us that they track the funds the agency pays to contractors to prepare NEPA analyses and does not track other costs, such as the time spent by DOE employees. According to DOE data, the average payment to a contractor to prepare an EIS from calendar year 2003 through calendar year 2012 was $6.6 million, with the range being a low of $60,000 and a high of $85 million.[24] DOE's median EIS contractor cost was $1.4 million over that time period. More recently, DOE's March 2014 NEPA quarterly report stated that for the 12 months that ended December 31, 2013, the median cost for the preparation of four EISs for which cost data were available was $1.7 million, and the average cost was $2.9 million. For context, a 2003 task force report to CEQ—the only available source of governmentwide cost estimates—estimated that an EIS typically cost from $250,000 to $2 million.[25]

In comparison, DOE's payments to contractors to produce an EA ranged from $3,000 to $1.2 million with a median cost of $65,000 from calendar year 2003 through calendar year 2012, according to DOE data. In its March 2014 NEPA quarterly report, DOE stated that, for the 12 months that ended December 31, 2013, the median cost for the preparation of 8 EAs was $73,000, and the average cost was $301,000. For governmentwide context, the 2003 task force report to CEQ estimated that an EA typically costs from $5,000 to $200,000.[26] Agencies provided no cost data on CEs but stated that the cost of a CE—which, in many cases, is for a "routine" activity, such as repainting a building—was generally much lower than the cost of an EA.

### *Some Information Is Available on NEPA Time Frames*

Some governmentwide information is available on time frames for completing EISs—which can be one element of project cost—but few estimates exist for EAs and CEs because most agencies do not collect information on the number and type of NEPA analyses, and few guidelines exist on time frames for completing environmental analyses (see app. III for information on CEQ NEPA time frame guidelines). NAEP annually reports information on EIS time frames by analyzing information published by agencies in the Federal Register, with the Notice of Intent to complete an EIS as the "start" date, and the Notice of Availability for the final EIS as the "end" date.[27] Our review did not identify other governmentwide sources of these data. Based on the information published in the Federal Register, NAEP reported in April 2013 that the 197 final EISs in 2012 had an average preparation time of 1,675 days, or 4.6 years—the highest average EIS preparation time the organization had recorded since 1997.[28] From 2000 through 2012, according to NAEP, the total annual average governmentwide EIS preparation time increased at an average rate of 34.2 days per year.[29]

In addition, some agency officials told us that time frame measures for EISs may not account for up-front work that occurs before the Notice of Intent to produce an EIS—the "start" date typically used in EIS time frame calculations. DOT officials told us that the "start" date is unclear in some cases because of the large volume of project development and planning work that occurs before a Notice of Intent is issued. DOE officials made a similar point, noting that time frames are difficult to determine for many NEPA analyses because there is a large volume of up-front work that is not captured by standard time frame measures. According to technical comments from CEQ and federal agencies, to ensure consistency in its NEPA metrics, DOE measures EIS completion time from the date of publication of the Notice of Intent to the date of publication of the notice of availability of the final EIS. Further, according to a 2007 CRS report, a project may stop and restart for any number of reasons that are unrelated to NEPA or any other environmental requirement.[30] For example, a 10- year time frame to complete a project may have been associated with funding issues, engineering requirements, changes in agency priorities, delays in obtaining nonfederal approvals, or community opposition to the project, to name a few.

Less governmentwide information is available on the completion time for EAs and CEs. According to DOE's June 2013 quarterly NEPA report, for the 12 months that ended March 31, 2013, the average completion time for 16 EAs was 13 months (with a median of 11 months). For the past 10 calendar years (i.e., 2003 through 2012), DOE's average EA completion time was 13 months (with a median of 9 months). Interior's Office of Surface Mining estimated that its EAs take approximately 4 months on average to complete, and the Forest Service reported that its 501 EAs in fiscal year 2012 took an average of about 18 months to complete. Further, officials from Bureau of Indian Affairs within Interior told us that their EAs are generally completed in about 1 month but that they may take up to 6 months depending on their complexity. In addition, DOT officials said that determining the start time of EAs and CEs is even more difficult than for EISs. The time for completing these can depend in large part on how much of the up-front work was done already as part of the preliminary engineering process and how many other environmental processes are involved (e.g., consultations under the Endangered Species Act).

The little governmentwide information that is available on CEs shows that they generally take less time to complete than EAs. DOE does not track completion times for CEs, but agency officials stated that they usually take 1 or 2 days. Similarly, officials at Interior's Office of Surface Mining reported that CEs take approximately 2 days to complete. In contrast, Forest Service took an average of 177 days to complete CEs in fiscal year 2012, shorter than its average of 565 days for EAs, according to agency documents. The Forest Service documents its CEs with Decision Memos, which are completed after all necessary consultations, reviews, and other determinations associated with a decision to implement a particular proposed project are completed.

## Information on the Benefits of Completing NEPA Analyses Is Largely Qualitative

According to agency officials, information on the benefits of completing NEPA analyses is largely qualitative. We have previously reported that assessing the benefits of federal environmental requirements, including those associated with NEPA, is difficult because the monetization of environmental benefits often requires making subjective decisions on key assumptions.[31] According to studies and agency officials, some of the qualitative benefits of NEPA include its role as a tool for encouraging transparency and public participation and in discovering and addressing the potential effects of a proposal in the early design stages to avoid problems that could end up taking more time and being more costly in the long run.

*Encouraging public participation.* NEPA is intended to help government make informed decisions, encourage the public to participate in those decisions, and make the government accountable for its decisions. Public participation is a central part of the NEPA process, allowing agencies to obtain input directly from those individuals who may be affected by a federal action. DOE officials referred to this public comment component of NEPA as a piece of "good government architecture," and DOD officials similarly described NEPA as a forum for resolving organizational differences by promoting interaction between interested parties inside and outside the government. Likewise, the National Park Service within Interior uses its Planning, Environment, and Public Comment (PEPC) system as a comprehensive information and public comment site for National Park Service projects, including those requiring NEPA analyses.[32]

*Discovering and addressing design problems.* One benefit of the environmental review process, according to a 2012 CRS report, is that it ultimately saves time and reduces overall project costs by identifying and avoiding problems that may occur in later stages of project development.[33] Projects that make it through the NEPA process are financially and environmentally improved, according to a senior NAEP official, because the process helps planners avoid the multiyear cost of mitigating a project's potential adverse effects up front by identifying and evaluating alternatives that would not otherwise have been identified. Moreover, agency officials who oversee federal NEPA programs told us that one of the benefits of NEPA analyses is that they lead to improved projects. For example, DOT officials stated that the NEPA process allows project decision makers to discover and solve design problems that could end up being more costly in the long run. Similarly, Forest Service officials said that NEPA leads to better decisions on projects because of the environmental information considered in the process. Providing examples to illustrate these points, CEQ published a document describing time savings and improved outcomes on projects funded by the Recovery Act. Similarly, NEPA Success Stories: Celebrating Forty Years of Transparency and Open Government—published in August 2010 as a joint effort by the Environmental Law Institute, the Grand Canyon Trust, and the Partnership Project—described and highlighted improved environmental outcomes brought about through the NEPA process.[34] DOE has also published a document showing its NEPA "success stories."[35] In one example from this document, DOE cited the November 28, 2008, Final Programmatic EIS for the Designation of Energy Corridors on Federal Lands in 11 Western States (DOE/EIS-0386), that it had developed in cooperation with BLM. In this case, public comments resulted in the consideration of alternative routes and operating procedures for energy transmission corridors to avoid sensitive environmental resources.

## Activities under NEPA Are Hard to Separate from Other Required Environmental Analyses, Complicating the Determination of Costs and Benefits

Agency activities under NEPA are hard to separate from other required environmental analyses, further complicating the determination of costs and benefits. CEQ's NEPA regulations specify that, to the fullest extent possible, agencies must prepare NEPA analyses concurrently with other environmental requirements. CEQ's March 6, 2012, memorandum on Improving the Process for Preparing Efficient and Timely Environmental Reviews under the National Environmental Policy Act states that agencies "must integrate, to the fullest extent possible, their draft EIS with environmental impact analyses and related surveys and studies required by other statutes or executive orders, amplifying the requirement in the CEQ regulations.[36] The goal should be to conduct concurrent rather than sequential processes whenever appropriate." Different types of environmental analyses may also be conducted in response to other requirements under federal laws such as the Clean Water Act and the Endangered Species Act; executive orders; agency guidance; and state and local laws. As reported in 2011 by CRS, NEPA functions as an "umbrella" statute; any study, review, or consultation required by any other law that is related to the environment should be conducted within the framework of the NEPA process.[37]

As a result, the biggest challenge in determining the costs and benefits of NEPA is separating activities under NEPA from activities under other environmental laws. According to DOT officials, the dollar costs for developing a NEPA analysis reported by agencies also includes costs for developing analyses required by a number of other federal laws, executive orders, and state and local laws, which potentially could be a significant part of the cost estimate. Similarly, DOD officials stated that NEPA is one piece of the larger environmental review process involving many environmental requirements associated with a project. As noted by officials from the Bureau of Reclamation within Interior, the NEPA process by design incorporates a multitude of other compliance issues and provides a framework and orderly process—akin to an assembly line— which can help reduce delays. In some instances, a delay in NEPA is the result of a delay in an ancillary effort to comply with another law, according to these officials and a wide range of other sources.

## Some Information Is Available on the Frequency and Outcome of NEPA Litigation

Some information is available on the frequency and outcome of NEPA litigation. Agency data, interviews with agency officials, and available studies indicate that most NEPA analyses do not result in litigation, although the impact of litigation could be substantial if a lawsuit affects numerous federal decisions or actions in several states. The federal government prevails in most NEPA litigation, according to CEQ and NAEP data, and legal studies.

## Available Data Show That Most NEPA Analyses Do Not Result in Litigation, but Individual Cases Can Have Substantial Impacts

Agency data, interviews with agency officials, and available studies indicate that most NEPA analyses do not result in litigation. While no governmentwide system exists to track NEPA litigation or its associated costs, NEPA litigation data are available from CEQ, the Department of Justice, and NAEP. Appendix IV describes how these sources gather information in different ways for different purposes.

The number of lawsuits filed under NEPA has generally remained stable following a decline after the early years of implementation, according to CEQ and other sources. NEPA litigation began to decline in the mid-1970s and has remained relatively constant since the late 1980s, as reported by CRS in 2007.[38] More specifically, 189 cases were filed in 1974, according to the twenty-fifth anniversary report of CEQ. In 1994, 106 NEPA lawsuits were filed. Since that time, according to CEQ data, the number of NEPA lawsuits filed annually has consistently been just above or below 100, with the exception of a period in the early- and mid-2000s.[39] In 2011, the most recent data available, CEQ reported 94 NEPA cases, down from the average of 129 cases filed per year from 2001 through 2008.[40] In 2012, U.S. Courts of Appeals issued 28 decisions involving implementation of NEPA by federal agencies, according to NAEP data.

Although the number of NEPA lawsuits is relatively small when compared with the total number of NEPA analyses, one lawsuit can affect numerous federal decisions or actions in several states, having a far-reaching impact. In addition to CEQ regulations and an agency's own regulations, according to a 2011 CRS report, preparers of NEPA analyses and documentation may be mindful of previous judicial interpretation in an attempt to prepare a "litigation-proof" EIS.[41] CEQ has observed that such an effort may lead to an increase in the cost and time needed to complete NEPA analyses but not necessarily to an improvement in the quality of the documents ultimately produced.

## The Federal Government Prevails in Most NEPA Litigation

The federal government prevails in most NEPA litigation, according to CEQ and NAEP data and other legal studies. CEQ annually publishes survey results on NEPA litigation that identify the number of cases involving a NEPA-based cause of action; federal agencies that were identified as a lead defendant; and general information on plaintiffs (i.e., grouped into categories, such as "public interest groups" and "business groups"); reasons for litigation; and outcomes of the cases decided during the year.[42] In general, according to CEQ data, NEPA case outcomes are about evenly split between those involving challenges to EISs and those involving other challenges to the adequacy of NEPA analyses (e.g., EAs and CEs). The federal government successfully defended its decisions in more than 50 percent of the cases from 2008 through 2011. For example, in 2011, 99 of the 146 total NEPA case dispositions—68 percent— reported by CEQ resulted in a judgment favorable to the federal agency being sued or a dismissal of the case without settlement.[43] In 2011, that rate increased to 80 percent if the 18 settlements reported by CEQ were considered successes.[44] However, the CEQ data do not present enough case-specific details to determine whether the settlements should be considered as favorable dispositions. The plaintiffs, in most cases, were public interest groups.

Reporting litigation outcome data similar to CEQ's, a January 2014 article on Forest Service land management litigation found that the Forest Service won nearly 54 percent of its cases and lost about 23 percent.[45] About 23 percent of the cases were settled, which the study found to be an important dispute resolution tool. Litigants generally challenged logging projects, most frequently under the National Environmental Policy Act and the National Forest Management Act. The article found that the Forest Service had a lower success rate in cases where plaintiffs advocated for less resource use (generally initiated by environmental groups) compared to cases where greater resource use was advocated. The report noted that environmental groups suing the Forest Service for less resource use not only have more potential statutory bases for legal challenges available to them than groups seeking more use of national forest resources, but there are also more statutes that relate directly to enhancing public participation and protecting natural resources.

Other sources of information also show that the federal government prevails in most NEPA litigation. For example, NAEP's 2012 annual NEPA report stated that the government prevailed in 24 of the 28 cases (86 percent) decided by U.S. Courts of Appeals. A NEPA legal treatise similarly reports that "government agencies almost always win their case when the adequacy of an EIS is challenged, if the environmental analysis is reasonably complete. Adequacy cases raise primarily factual issues on which the courts normally defer to the agency. The success record in litigation is more evenly divided when a NEPA case raises threshold questions that determine whether the agency has complied with the statute. An example is a challenge to an agency decision that an EIS was not required. Some lower federal courts are especially sensitive to agency attempts to avoid their NEPA responsibilities."[46] NAEP also provides detailed descriptions of cases decided by U.S. Courts of Appeals in its annual reports.[47]

## AGENCY COMMENTS AND OUR EVALUATION

We provided a draft of this product to the Council on Environmental Quality (CEQ) for governmentwide comments in coordination with the Departments of Agriculture, Defense, Energy, Interior, Justice, and Transportation, and the Environmental Protection Agency (EPA). In written comments CEQ generally agreed with our findings. CEQ and federal agencies also provided technical comments that we incorporated, as appropriate.

Anne-Marie Fennell
Director, Natural Resources and Environment

Alfredo Gomez
Director, Natural Resources and Environment

Brian Lepore
Director, Defense Capabilities and Management

## APPENDIX I. OBJECTIVES, SCOPE, AND METHODOLOGY

This appendix provides information on the scope of work and the methodology used to collect information on how we described the (1) number and type of National Environmental Policy Act (NEPA) analyses, (2) costs and benefits of completing those analyses, and (3) frequency and outcomes of related litigation. We included available information on both costs and benefits to be consistent with standard economic principles for evaluating federal programs and generally accepted government auditing standards.

To respond to these objectives, we reviewed relevant publications, obtained documents and analyses from federal agencies, and interviewed federal officials and individuals from academia and a professional association with expertise in conducting NEPA analyses. Specifically, to describe the number and type of NEPA analyses and what is known about the costs and benefits of NEPA analyses, we reported information identified through the literature review, interviews, and other sources. We selected the Departments of Defense, Energy, the Interior, and Transportation and the Forest Service within the U.S. Department of Agriculture for analysis because they generally complete the most NEPA analyses. Our findings for these agencies are not generalizeable to other federal agencies.

To assess the availability of information to respond to these objectives, we (1) conducted a literature search and review with the assistance of a technical librarian; (2) reviewed our past work on NEPA and studies from the Congressional Research Service; (3) obtained documents and analyses from federal agencies; and (4) interviewed officials who oversee federal NEPA programs from the Departments of Defense, Energy, the Interior, Justice, and Transportation; the Forest Service within the Department of Agriculture; the Environmental Protection Agency (EPA); the Council on Environmental Quality (CEQ) within the Executive Office of the President; and individuals with expertise from academia and the National Association of Environmental Professionals (NAEP)—a professional association representing private and government NEPA practitioners.

Specifically, to describe the number and type of NEPA analyses from calendar year 2008 through calendar year 2012, we analyzed data identified through the literature review and interviews. We focused on data and documents maintained by CEQ, EPA, and NAEP. CEQ and NAEP periodically report data on the number of certain types of NEPA analyses, and EPA maintains a database of Environmental Impact Statements, one of its roles in implementing NEPA. To generate information on the number of Environmental Impact Statements from EPA's database, we sorted the data by calendar year and counted the number of analyses for each year. We did not conduct an extensive evaluation of this database, although a high-level analysis discovered potential inconsistencies. For example, EPA's database contained entries with the same unique identifier, making it difficult to identify the exact number of NEPA analyses. We discussed these inconsistencies with EPA officials, who told us that they were aware of certain errors due to manual data entry and the use of different analysis methods. These officials said that EPA EIS data provided to others may differ because EPA periodically corrects the manually entered data. We did not count duplicate records in our analysis of EPA's data. We believe these data are sufficiently reliable for the purposes of this report.

To describe what is known about the costs and benefits of NEPA analysis, we reported the available information on the subject identified through the literature review and interviews. To describe the frequency and outcome of NEPA litigation we (1) reviewed laws, regulations, and agency guidance; (2) reviewed NEPA litigation data generated by CEQ and NAEP; (3) interviewed Department of Justice officials; and (4) reviewed relevant legal studies.

Information from these sources is cited in footnotes throughout this report. To answer the various objectives, we relied on data from several sources. To assess the reliability of data collected by agencies and NAEP, we reviewed existing documentation, when available, and interviewed officials knowledgeable about the data. We found all data sufficiently reliable for the purposes of this report.

We conducted this performance audit from June 2013 to April 2014 in accordance with generally accepted government auditing standards. Those standards require that we plan and perform the audit to obtain sufficient, appropriate evidence to provide a reasonable basis for our findings and conclusions based on our audit objectives. We believe that the evidence obtained provides a reasonable basis for our findings and conclusions based on our audit objectives.

# Appendix II. Summary of Federal NEPA Data Collection Efforts

Federal National Environmental Policy Act (NEPA) data collection efforts vary by agency. The Council on Environmental Quality's (CEQ) NEPA implementing regulations set forth requirements that federal agencies must adhere to, and require federal agencies to adopt their own procedures, as necessary, that conform with NEPA and CEQ's regulations.[48] Federal agencies decide how to apply CEQ regulations in the NEPA process. According to a 2007 Congressional Research Service (CRS) report, the CEQ regulations were meant to be generic in nature, with individual agencies formulating procedures applicable to their own projects.[49] The report states that this approach was taken because of the diverse nature of projects and environmental impacts managed by federal agencies with unique mandates and missions. Consequently, NEPA procedures vary to some extent from agency to agency, and comprehensive governmentwide data on NEPA analyses are generally not centrally collected.

As stated by a CEQ official, "there is no master NEPA spreadsheet, and there are many gaps in NEPA-related data collected across the federal government." To obtain information on agency NEPA activities, the official said that CEQ works closely with its federal agency NEPA contact group, composed of key officials responsible for implementing NEPA in each agency. CEQ meets regularly with these officials and uses this network to collect NEPA-related information through requests for information, whereby CEQ distributes a list of questions to relevant agencies and then collects and reports the answers. According to CEQ officials, NEPA data reported by CEQ are generated through these requests, which have quality assurance limitations because related activities at federal departments are themselves diffused throughout various offices.

Of the agencies we reviewed, the Departments of Defense, the Interior, and Transportation do not centrally collect information on NEPA analyses, allowing component agencies to collect the information, whereas the Department of Energy and the Forest Service within the Department of Agriculture aggregate certain data.

*Department of Defense (DOD).* Each of the military services and defense agencies collects data on NEPA analyses, but DOD does not aggregate information that is collected on the number and type of NEPA analyses at the departmentwide level. Data collection within the military services and agencies is decentralized, according to DOD officials. For example, the Army collects Environmental Impact Statement (EIS) data at the Armywide level, and responsibility for Environmental Assessments (EA) and Categorical Exclusions (CE) are delegated to the lowest possible command level. DOD officials said that each of the services and defense agencies works to maintain a balance between the work that needs to be completed and the management effort needed to accomplish that work. While the level of information collected may vary by service or defense agency, each collects the information that it has determined necessary to manage its NEPA workload. According to these officials, every new information system and data call must generally come from existing funding, taking resources from other tasks.

*Department of the Interior (Interior).* Data are not collected at the department level, according to Interior officials, and Interior conducts its own departmentwide data calls to component bureaus and entities whenever CEQ asks for NEPA-related information. The data collection efforts of its individual bureaus vary considerably. For example, the National Park Service uses its

Planning, Environment, and Public Comment (PEPC) system as a comprehensive information and public comment site for National Park Service projects. Other Interior bureaus are beginning to track information or rely on less formal systems and not formalized databases. For example, the Bureau of Indian Affairs uses its internal NEPA Tracker system—started in September 2012—which the bureau states is to collect information on NEPA analyses to create a better administrative record to potentially identify new categories of CEs for future development and use. Prior to the NEPA Tracker system, the Bureau of Indian Affairs tracked NEPA analyses less formally, with varying information quality across the bureau's different entities, according to agency officials. According to Bureau of Land Management officials, the bureau has developed and is currently implementing its ePlanning system, a comprehensive, bureau-wide, Internet-based tool for writing, reviewing, publishing, and receiving public commentary on land use plans and NEPA documents. The tool is fully operational, and the bureau expects to complete implementation in 2015. At the Bureau of Reclamation, NEPA activities are cataloged and tracked by each region or area office according to local procedures, and the information on the number and type of NEPA analyses resides with these offices. NEPA information at the Fish and Wildlife Service, according to agency officials, is collected at the refuge level.

*Department of Transportation (DOT).* According to agency officials, each DOT administration—such as the Federal Highway Administration (FHWA), which funds highway projects; the Federal Motor Carrier Safety Administration, which develops commercial motor vehicle and driver regulations; and the Federal Aviation Administration, which is responsible for, among other things, the nation's air traffic control system—has its own NEPA operating and data collection procedures that track NEPA- related information to varying degrees because each mode of transportation has different characteristics and needs.[50] Environmental reviews for highway projects funded by FHWA have long been of interest to Congress and federal, state, and local stakeholders.[51] FHWA and its 52 division offices have traditionally used an internal data system to track EIS documents. FHWA officials told us that they are in the process of replacing the agency's legacy system with the new Project and Program Action Information (PAPAI) system, which went online in March 2013. PAPAI is capable of tracking information on EISs, EAs, and CEs, including project completion time frames, but its use is not mandatory, according to DOT officials.

*Department of Energy (DOE).* The Office of NEPA Policy and Compliance within DOE maintains a website where it posts extensive agencywide NEPA documentation, including information on the number and type of NEPA analyses completed since the mid-1990s and a series of quarterly lessons learned reports documenting certain NEPA performance metrics, including information on time and cost.[52] DOE's September 2013 quarterly report documents available information on its NEPA analysis workload, completion times, and costs from 2003 through 2012.[53] DOE began tracking cost and completion time metrics in the mid-1990s because it was concerned about the timeliness and cost of NEPA reviews.[54] DOE officials told us they collect these data because, in their view, "what gets measured gets done." Making DOE NEPA analyses easily available allows others to apply the best practices and potentially avoid costly litigation, according to DOE officials.

*Department of Agriculture's Forest Service*. The Forest Service's computer system, known as the Planning, Appeals, and Litigation System, provides information for responding to congressional requests for NEPA data, to support preparation for responding to lawsuits, and about overall project objectives and design. As stated by agency officials, data from the system can be used to identify trends in the preparation of NEPA analyses over time. This information can be valuable to managers in managing overall NEPA compliance and can identify innovative ways to deal with recurring environmental issues that affect projects, according to Forest Service officials. The system also provides tools to help the agency meet NEPA requirements, including automatic distribution of the schedule of proposed NEPA actions, a searchable database of draft EISs, and electronic filing of draft and final EISs to EPA.

CEQ also identified as a best practice the service's electronic Management of NEPA (eMNEPA) pilot—a suite of web-based tools and databases to improve the efficiency of environmental reviews by enabling online submission and processing of public comments, among other things.[55] On March 17, 2011, CEQ invited members of the public and federal agencies to nominate projects employing innovative approaches to complete environmental reviews more efficiently and effectively. On August 31, 2011, CEQ announced that eMNEPA was selected as part of the first NEPA pilot project. CEQ officials told us that they would prioritize the use of CEQ oversight resources to focus on identifying, disseminating, and encouraging agencies to use their additional resources in improving operational efficiency through tools like eMNEPA rather than focusing on improved data collection and reporting. Specifically, CEQ officials said that information technology tools that enable easy access to relevant technical information across the federal government are also of value in enhancing the ability of agencies to conduct efficient and timely NEPA environmental reviews.

# APPENDIX III. CEQ NEPA TIME FRAME GUIDELINES

The Council on Environmental Quality's (CEQ) March 1981 guidance document published in the Federal Register titled Forty Most Asked Questions Concerning CEQ's National Environmental Policy Act Regulations advises that

> "... even large complex energy projects would require only about 12 months for the completion of the entire EIS process. For most major actions, this period is well within the planning time that is needed in any event, apart from NEPA. The time required for the preparation of program EISs may be greater. The Council also recognizes that some projects will entail difficult long-term planning and/or the acquisition of certain data which of necessity will require more time for the preparation of the EIS. Indeed, some proposals should be given more time for the thoughtful preparation of an EIS and development of a decision which fulfills NEPA's substantive goals. For cases in which only an environmental assessment will be prepared, the NEPA process should take no more than 3 months, and in many cases substantially less, as part of the normal analysis and approval process for the action."[56]

CEQ's National Environmental Policy Act (NEPA) regulations do not specify a required time frame for completing NEPA analyses. The regulations state that CEQ has decided that prescribed universal time limits for the entire NEPA process are too inflexible. The regulations also state that federal agencies are encouraged to set time limits appropriate to individual actions and should take into consideration factors such as the potential for environmental harm, size of the proposed action, and degree of public need for the proposed action, including the consequences of delay. CEQ's March 6, 2012, memorandum on Improving the Process for Preparing Efficient and Timely Environmental Reviews under the National Environmental Policy Act encourages agencies to develop meaningful and expeditious timelines for environmental reviews, and it amplifies the factors an agency should take into account when setting time limits, noting that establishing appropriate and predictable time limits promotes the efficiency of the NEPA process. The CEQ regulations also require agencies to reduce delay by, among other things, integrating the NEPA process into early project planning, emphasizing interagency cooperation, integrating NEPA requirements with other environmental review requirements, and adopting environmental documents prepared by other federal agencies.

# APPENDIX IV. SOURCES OF NEPA LITIGATION DATA

In general, there is no governmentwide system to track National Environmental Policy Act (NEPA) litigation and its associated costs. The Council on Environmental Quality (CEQ), the Department of Justice, and the National Association of Environmental Professionals (NAEP) gather NEPA litigation information in different ways for different purposes.

CEQ collects NEPA litigation data through periodic requests for information, whereby it distributes a list of questions to the general counsel offices of relevant agencies and then collects and reports the information on its website.[57] CEQ's NEPA litigation survey presents information on NEPA-based claims brought against agencies in court, including aggregated information on types of lawsuits and who brought the suits. The survey results do not present information on the cost of NEPA litigation because, according to officials from several of the agencies we reviewed, agencies do not track this information. For example, Forest Service officials told us that they do not centrally track the cost or time associated with the preparation for litigation. As another example, the Department of Energy's litigation data do not include the cost of litigation or the time spent on litigation-related tasks, although it includes the number of NEPA-related cases over time.

The Department of Justice defends nearly all federal agencies when they face NEPA litigation.[58] These officials told us that the department's Case Management System database tracks limited information on NEPA cases handled by the Environment and Natural Resources Division, and the Executive Office for U.S. Attorneys case management system, called the Legal Information Office Network System, tracks NEPA cases at individual U.S. Attorneys' Offices to some extent. However, Department of Justice officials told us that these systems do not interface with each other, so it would be impossible to gather comprehensive information on NEPA litigation from the Department of Justice.

Further, Department of Justice officials told us that the department is not able to comprehensively identify all NEPA litigation because a single case could have numerous other environmental claims in addition to a single NEPA claim. In such instances, the Environment and Natural Resources Division's Case Management System may not capture every claim raised in the case.[59] As a result, the Department of Justice does not track trends in NEPA litigation or staff hours spent on NEPA cases. The cost of collecting the information would outweigh the management benefits of doing so, according to these officials.

The Department of Justice's NEPA litigation data are not comparable to CEQ's because the department's system is designed to track cases, while CEQ provides information on NEPA events—such as the number of cases filed, number of injunctions or remands, and other decisions. There could be multiple NEPA events or decisions related to a single case. Department of Justice officials stated that they would not be able to reconcile CEQ's information with information in Department of Justice systems.

NEPA litigation data collected by the third source—NAEP—differ from those collected by CEQ or the Department of Justice. NAEP collects information on NEPA cases decided by U.S. Courts of Appeals because these cases are generally the most significant to the NEPA practitioners that are NAEP's members, according to NAEP officials. The NAEP report contains case study summaries of the latest developments in NEPA litigation to help NEPA practitioners understand how to account for new court-mandated requirements in NEPA analyses and does not attempt to track all NEPA litigation across the government.

## End Notes

[1] NEPA applies to federal agency policies, programs, plans, and projects (40 C.F.R. § 1508.18(b)). The focus of this report is on development projects.

[2] Pub. L. No. 91-190 (1970), codified at 42 U.S.C. § 4321-4347. NEPA's congressional declaration of purpose states that the purposes of the act are "to declare a national policy which will encourage productive and enjoyable harmony between man and his environment; to promote efforts which will prevent or eliminate damage to the environment and biosphere and stimulate the health and welfare of man; to enrich the understanding of the ecological systems and natural resources important to the Nation; and to establish a Council on Environmental Quality." 42 U.S.C. § 4321.

[3] The CEQ "Regulations for Implementing the Procedural Provisions of the National Environmental Policy Act" (CEQ regulations), 40 C.F.R. Parts 1500-1508, set out the levels of analysis and documentation for complying with NEPA. The level of analysis and documentation can take the form of a Categorical Exclusion (CE), Environmental Assessment (EA), or Environmental Impact Statement (EIS). Not all CEs are documented at the time the CE is used for a specific proposed project.

[4] The human environment is interpreted comprehensively to include the natural and physical environment and the relationship of people to that environment (40 C.F.R. § 1508.14). The effects analyzed under NEPA include ecological, aesthetic, historic, cultural, economic, social, or health (40 C.F.R. § 1508.8).

[5] An EIS must, among other things, (1) describe the environment that will be affected, (2) identify alternatives to the proposed action and identify the agency's preferred alternative, (3) present the environmental impacts of the proposed action and alternatives, and (4) identify any adverse environmental impacts that cannot be avoided should the proposed action be implemented.

[6] Some categorical exclusions are established by statute and therefore generally do not require an agency determination that such actions do not have a significant environmental impact.

[7] 40 C.F.R. § 1506.5.

[8] 40 C.F.R. Parts 1500-1508.

[9] The EIS process begins with publication of a Notice of Intent stating an agency intends to prepare an EIS for a proposed project. EPA publishes Notices of Availability in the *Federal Register* notifying the public when a draft EIS is available for comment and when a final EIS is has been issued.

[10] While there is no corresponding requirement for an EA public comment period, agencies may provide one. See, e.g., 40 C.F.R. § 1506.6 (Agencies shall make "diligent efforts to involve the public in preparing and implementing their NEPA procedures.")

[11] 40 CFR § 1502.9(c)(1).

[12] See 40 C.F.R. §§ 1500.4, 1500.5, and regulations cited therein.

[13] Also, unlike these other laws, while NEPA imposes procedural requirements, it does not establish substantive standards.

[14] CRS, *The National Environmental Policy Act (NEPA): Background and Implementation,* RL33152 (Washington, D.C.: Jan. 10, 2011). NEPA does not contain civil or criminal enforcement provisions; litigation challenging an agency's compliance is brought under the Administrative Procedure Act.

[15] The Recovery Act required the President to report to the Senate Environment and Public Works Committee and the House Natural Resources Committee every 90 days until September 30, 2011 on the status and progress of projects and activities funded by this Act with respect to compliance with National Environmental Policy Act requirements and documentation. Pub. L. No. 111-5, § 1609(c), 123 Stat. 304 (2009). Recovery Act projects may not be representative of ratios for all NEPA analyses. CEQ reports to Congress on the status and progress of NEPA reviews under the Recovery Act can be accessed at http://energy.gov/nepa/american-recovery-and-reinvestment-act-2009-and-nepa-ceq-reports-congress.

[16] CRS, *The National Environmental Policy Act (NEPA): Background and Implementation,* RL33152 (Washington, D.C.: Jan. 10, 2011).

[17] GAO, *Highway Projects: Some Federal and State Practices to Expedite Completion Show Progress,* GAO-12-593 (Washington, D.C.: June 6, 2012).

[18] NAEP's *annual NEPA reports generally include two sets of EIS data. The first set, presented in tables 1 and 2, reflects NAEP's analysis of the number of draft and final EIS announcements published in the Federal Register*. The second set of EIS data are used by NAEP to analyze the time frames associated with completing EISs. The two sets of EIS data within NAEP reports generally do not match, in part because the sample of EISs used to evaluate time frames excludes certain projects, such as "adoptions" or EISs that were subsequently supplemented.

[19] CRS, *The National Environmental Policy Act (NEPA): Background and Implementation,* RL33152 (Washington, D.C.: Jan. 10, 2011).

[20] NAEP, *Annual NEPA Report 2012 of the National Environmental Policy Act (NEPA) Practice* (April 2013).

[21] The agency remains responsible for the scope and content of the analyses under NEPA and the NEPA documentation. 40 C.F.R. § 1506.5.

[22] U.S. Forest Service, Competitive Sourcing Program Office, *Feasibility Study of Activities Related to National Environmental Policy Act (NEPA) Compliance* (Washington, D.C.: Aug. 10, 2007).

[23] U.S. Department of Transportation, Federal Highway Administration, *Evaluating the Performance of Environmental Streamlining: Phase II* (Washington, D.C.: 2003). We have ongoing work reviewing what is known about any duplication resulting from state and federal environmental impact review requirements for federal highway projects, as required by Section 1322 of the Moving Ahead for Progress in the 21st Century Act, Pub. L. No. 112-141, 126 Stat. 405, 553 (2012). We expect to issue a final report by the end of October 2014.

[24] According to DOE, the cost for the $85 million Hanford Tank Closure and Waste Management EIS includes the costs for three major EISs—waste management, high-level waste tank closure, and disposition of a nuclear reactor—that were started separately and ultimately integrated into one document.

[25] The NEPA Task Force Report to The Council on Environmental Quality, *Modernizing NEPA Implementation.* (September 2003).

[26] The NEPA Task Force Report to The Council on Environmental Quality, *Modernizing NEPA Implementation.* (September 2003). This report estimated that a "small" EA typically costs from $5,000 to $20,000 and a "large" EA costs from $50,000 to $200,000, but the report did not define "small" and "large."

[27] According to CEQ officials, time frame data do not reflect certain nuances in the NEPA process. There could be a number of "non-NEPA" reasons for the "start," "pause," and "stop" of a project, such as waiting for funding or a non-federal permit, authorization, or other determination.

[28] NAEP, *Annual NEPA Report 2012 of the National Environmental Policy Act (NEPA) Practice* (April 2013). NAEP's estimates are subject to sampling error and highlight the considerable variability in the time frames associated with EISs across the federal government. NAEP presented its time frame data along with margins of error at one standard deviation. NAEP's NEPA average preparation time of 1,675 days had a one standard deviation confidence interval of plus or minus 1,247 days (plus or minus 3.4 years). Also, the number of final EISs included in this sample—197—does not match the number of final EISs—210—presented for 2012 in table 1. NAEP's annual reports use two different sources of information on NEPA analyses, one for its count of NEPA analysis, and another for analyzing time frames.

[29] For more information on EIS time frames, see Piet deWitt and Carole A. deWitt, "How Long Does It Take to Prepare an Environmental Impact Statement?" *Environmental Practice* 10, no. 4 (December 2008) and Piet deWitt and Carole A. deWitt, "Preparation Times for Final Environmental Impact Statements Made Available from 2007 through 2010," *Environmental Practice* 15, no. 2 (June 2013).

[30] CRS, *The National Environmental Policy Act: Streamlining NEPA,* RL33267 (Washington, D.C.: Dec. 6, 2007).

[31] GAO, *Federal-Aid Highways: Federal Requirements for Highways May Influence Funding Decisions and Create Challenges, but Benefits and Costs Are Not Tracked,* GAO-09-36 (Washington, D.C.: December 12, 2008).

[32] Visit http://parkplanning.nps.gov/ for more information on PEPC.

[33] CRS, *The Role of the Environmental Review Process in Federally Funded Highway Projects: Background and Issues for Congress,* R42479, (Washington, D.C.: Apr. 11, 2012).

[34] Visit http://energy.gov/nepa/nepa-success-stories-and-benefits to see "NEPA Success Stories and Benefits." As of February 26, 2014, CEQ's NEPA.gov website was down due to security issues.

[35] DOE's NEPA success stories can be found at http://energy.gov/nepa/downloads/nepa-success-stories-lessons-learned-quarterly-reports-0.

[36] 40 C.F.R. Parts 1500-1508, at § 1502.25.

[37] CRS, *The National Environmental Policy Act (NEPA): Background and Implementation,* RL33152 (Washington, D.C.: Jan. 10, 2011). According to technical comments from CEQ and federal agencies, this statement is overbroad. Studies, reviews, or consultations required

by law and related to the environment may occur outside the NEPA process when necessary, and in fact this routinely occurs in real practice. Thus, according to the technical comments, it would be more accurate to track the language in the relevant CEQ regulation, 40 CFR 1500.2(c).

[38] CRS, *The National Environmental Policy Act: Streamlining NEPA,* RL33267 (Washington, D.C.: Dec. 6, 2007).

[39] As summarized by CEQ on its website, since 2001, fewer than 175 NEPA cases were filed each year, with fewer than 100 filed each year in 2007, 2009, 2010, and 2011. A 2004 report by the Environmental Law Institute cited an increase in the number of NEPA cases filed in 2001 and 2002. See Jay E. Austin, et al. *Judging NEPA: A "Hard Look" at Judicial Decision Making Under the National Environmental Policy Act* (Washington, D.C.: Environmental Law Institute, 2004).

[40] Steven K. Imig, NEPA Case Law Update, *Rocky Mountain Mineral Law Foundation Special Institute on the National Environmental Policy Act,* October 28-29, 2010, Paper 12.

[41] CRS, *The National Environmental Policy Act (NEPA): Background and Implementation,* RL33152 (Washington, D.C.: Jan. 10, 2011).

[42] CEQ did not define the terms "public interest group" or "business group" in its published survey results. According to CEQ officials, CEQ used the terms "public interest group" to include citizen groups and environmental nongovernmental organizations and the term "business group" to include business, industry, and development focused groups and organizations.

[43] The total number of dispositions does not relate directly to the 94 cases filed in 2011 because litigation may take multiple years to resolve and there may be more than one disposition per case.

[44] The CEQ surveys identify three types of nonadverse dispositions: (1) judgment for the defendant; (2) dismissal without settlement; and (3) settlement.

[45] Amanda M.A. Miner, Robert W. Mamsheimer, and Denise M. Keele, "Twenty Years of Forest Service Land Management Litigation," *Journal of Forestry* 112, no. 1 (January 2014).

[46] Daniel R. Mandelker, with the assistance of Robert L. Glicksman, Arianne Michalek Aughey, JD, and Donald McGillivray, *NEPA Law and Litigation*, 2nd ed. (Thomson Reuters/West, Rel. 10, 2012).

[47] NAEP, *Annual NEPA Report 2012 of the National Environmental Policy Act (NEPA) Practice* (April 2013).

[48] 40 C.F.R. § 1507.3.

[49] CRS, *The National Environmental Policy Act: Streamlining NEPA,* RL33267 (Washington, D.C.: Dec. 6, 2007).

[50] According to technical comments from CEQ and federal agencies, several DOT administrations, including Federal Aviation Administration, are tracking the status of NEPA analyses, or NEPA status is reported as part of a larger financial tracking database.

[51] GAO-12-593.

[52] Visit http://energy.gov/nepa/office-nepa-policy-and-compliance to see the information on DOE's website.

[53] DOE's September 2013 quarterly report can be found at http://energy.gov/nepa/downloads/lessons-learned-quarterly-report-september-2013. These data are discussed in more detail elsewhere in this report.

[54] DOE, *Secretarial Policy Statement on the National Environmental Policy Act*, (Washington, D.C.: June 13, 1994). The secretarial policy statement is available at http://energy.gov/nepa/downloads/doe-secretarial-policy-statement-national-environmental-policy-act.

[55] More information on Forest Service's eMNEPA is available at at http://www.eforest.us/group/emnepa.

[56] CEQ, *Memorandum to Agencies: Forty Most Asked Questions Concerning CEQ's National Environmental Policy Act Regulations*. 46 Fed. Reg. 18026 (Mar. 23, 1981) as amended.

[57] CEQ used to report on NEPA litigation in required annual reports, but the annual reporting requirement was eliminated by Congress, and the last annual report was issued in 1997. CEQ's more recent NEPA litigation survey results are provided at http://energy.gov/nepa/downloads/nepa-litigation-surveys.

[58] Such litigation is handled both by the Department of Justice's Environment and Natural Resources Division and by individual U.S. Attorneys' Offices depending upon the agency, the type of case, and the expertise of the department's personnel. Agency personnel provide the Department of Justice with the administrative record that forms the basis of judicial review and provide assistance throughout the litigation process, as needed.

[59] According to Department of Justice officials, the Environment and Natural Resources Division uses a customized Case Management System for internal purposes. This Case Management System includes case information such as the caption, lead statute, court district, case hours, and general outcomes. The Environment and Natural Resources Division generally uses the Case Management System information to measure performance, assess resource needs and expenditures, and track the hours of certain employees to individual cases.

# INDEX

## D



## E

## O



## P



## Q



## R

## S



## T



## U



## W